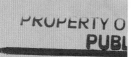

CONTENTS

About FindRugbyNow

This book would not have been possible without FindRugbyNow, a London based rugby company. The authors of this book met through their involvement with the company and each of them continues to write articles for its website on a regular basis.

FindRugbyNow (FRN) was founded in 2011 with a dual purpose: one, to provide quality content focussed on amateur rugby to rugby enthusiasts and two, to build local rugby communities by bringing together rugby clubs, players, coaches, referees and fans.

Authors Dave Beal, Ellaine Gelman and Ian Milligan

FRN's website (www.findrugbynow.com) offers searches for rugby clubs, shops and locations to watch rugby matches in local communities and encourages rugger interaction through a fixture exchange, marketplace and classifieds section. FRN also provides a calendar of upcoming local rugby events and tournaments and information about local rugby clubs.

In addition to the above, the site offers a rugby blog for rugby enthusiasts, including content on fitness and conditioning, common rugby injuries, rugby nutrition, mini and youth rugby, coaching strategies, inside looks at the life of professional players (written by professional players and internationals), women's rugby and more!

FRN also focuses on providing quality mini and youth rugby content targeted at coaches, parents and referees, which can be found on its sister site www.miniandyouthrugby.com. Check out this webpage for regular articles outlining rule changes, changes to the game and useful coaching advice, amongst other things. You can also contact the authors if you have any questions or comments.

FRN also hosts a large rugby festival in the summertime (www.sevenstournament.com) as well as smaller rugby tournaments throughout the year in the London area.

If you are a player, club, bloggers, photographer or any other type of rugby lover interested in getting involved, please get in touch today and become a part of the FRN team.

You can reach FRN in the following ways:

Email – admin@findrugbynow.com
Facebook – https://www.facebook.com/findrugbynow
Twitter – https://twitter.com/FindRugbyNow
LinkedIn – https://uk.linkedin.com/pub/find-rugby-now/46/190/b2

INTRODUCTION

There has never been a more exciting time to be a rugby player. Following the inclusion of rugby 7s as an Olympic sport into the 2016 Olympics in Rio, rugby has been front and centre on the world stage. This has prompted many countries to invest substantially in both the men's and women's 7s game, which has undoubtedly benefited the rugby sport as a whole, with even non-traditional rugby nations like the United States starting to invest in the future of the sport. This has had the biggest impact on the women's game, which now boasts professional players who are paid to travel the world and compete in international tournaments.

For both the men's and women's game, the quality of the rugby 7s professional athletes is filtering into the 15s game, since most players continue to play club rugby throughout the year and sometimes also represent their countries in the 15s game. The popularity of the 7s game has also led to an increase of interest in the sport by many countries, including non-traditional rugby countries like Afghanistan, Iraq and Brazil.

According to the Rugby Football Union (RFU), rugby is the fastest-growing sport in the UK, attracting more people than ever in the form of players, spectators and club volunteers. In 2014, the Rugby World Cup was the third largest global sporting event in the world behind the Olympic Games and the FIFA World Cup.

The success of the Women's Rugby World Cup in August 2014, which saw England Women crowned world champions, has also led to many nations capitalising on the growing popularity of the women's game. This has included initiatives such as the Irish Rugby Football Union's 'Give it a Try' scheme, to assist those interested in developing Girls Minis rugby teams across the country.[1]

In September 2014, the RFU announced plans to introduce rugby to 100,000 women and girls across the country. According to the RFU, it 'aims to grow the game to see 25,000 women and girls taking part in contact rugby by 2017, while expanding the reach of the game to attract more coaches, volunteers, officials, social players and fans'.[2]

Signs of the growing interest have been evidenced with the growth of the women and girls' game between 2013 and 2014, with playing numbers increasing from 15,000 to 18,000 – double the growth seen in any other year.[3]

Stepping away from rugby 7s and 15s, touch rugby leagues and competitions are now more popular than ever in the UK, with the backing of corporate sponsorship. This has provided an opportunity for both men and women who are new to the sport to enjoy some of its benefits in a social environment and allowed senior players to continue playing rugby well into their adult years. In 2014, 8000 players took part in the O2 Touch leagues.

At the same time, rugby is now more scrutinised than ever. The University of London's Professor of Public Health Research and Policy, Allyson Pollock, stated on Sky Sports News in February 2014 that it must 'become a very different game from the very brutal game that we are seeing the professional players play' and called for a ban on rugby.

These issues are not new to rugby. In fact, in 2010 an article in the *Guardian* questioned whether scrums should be banned in schools, citing research backed by £500,000 from the International Rugby Board (IRB, now World Rugby)[4]. The research was conducted by Professor Pollock, then Director of Edinburgh University's Centre for International Public Health Policy. A *Guardian* poll relating to that article saw 17 per cent of readers vote for and 83 per cent against banning scrums in schools.

Although Pollock is still in the minority, concerns over the safety of the sport, combined with the increase of coverage flowing from the upcoming Olympics, mean it is more important than ever that the rugby community addresses health and safety and coaching concerns and finds a way to continue to increase the sport's appeal to boys and girls of all ages.

There are few sports that include as many variations as rugby – rugby union, rugby league, 7s rugby, touch rugby, tag rugby, beach rugby, wheelchair rugby. There is something for everyone!

However, the fundamentals for all of these variations are very much the same – running good lines, working as part of a team, passing and catching the ball, communication and the ability to read the game.

It is for this reason that it is so important that we provide players with the right basics – so whatever form of rugby they choose to pursue, they will have all the skills and the knowledge to excel.

Furthermore, we must address the safety concerns highlighted in studies such as those of Professor Pollock by teaching players proper tackling techniques, educating coaches, parents and players about concussion, and ensuring that the game of rugby continues to maintain the right ethos.

I firmly agree with former England Rugby and British Lions player Will Greenwood, who responded to Professor Pollock's call to ban the sport in the following way:

> 'I am not immune to the worries of a parent – worrying that my boy Archie may pick up an injury along the way through rugby … [but] what rugby gives you is … the values that we hold dear in sport: respect, leadership, that ability to stand side by side. To me that is far more important than the occasional niggle and the occasional scrape.'

We hope this book will provide both parents and coaches with knowledge about the game, and introduce them to new coaching techniques – but most importantly, we hope that it conveys the importance of setting the right ethos, which (a) encourages young players to take up the sport and (b) ensures that players continue to play rugby as they get older. Please note that the information in this book is based on age grade rugby in the United Kingdom; readers outside the UK should check with their own Union for any differences in the rules for age grade players.

The ethos of rugby – the values that Greenwood describes – is what makes the sport so special and our dedication to this ethos as parents, coaches, managers, spectators and players is the only way that the sport can truly succeed.

Ellaine Gelman
Founder of FindRugbyNow

1 CREATING THE RIGHT ETHOS FOR MINIS AND YOUTH TEAMS

The central tenet of rugby is that it is a sport that is not just about knocking people down, it's also about building them up – and rugby coaches and parents are a key part of this equation.

To those who have played rugby for most of their lives, it is not an exaggeration to say that rugby is a way of life and many live by its code of conduct both on and off the pitch. When taught properly with the right ethos, rugby can play a big role in giving players skills that they can use throughout their lives, well beyond their playing days.

What is amazing is that a rugby player can turn up to any rugby club in any country in the world with a pair of rugby boots and they will be welcomed to take part. This, along with the fact that rugby players vary in shape and size, is a great example of the inclusive nature of the sport.

Values and the ethos of rugby

In England, the Rugby Football Union (RFU) has set out a Code of Rugby[5] and five core values to define its value system in formal terms and anyone involved in the sport (including players, coaches, referees, administrators, parents and spectators) is expected to uphold these values.

The Code of Rugby is as follows:

Play to win – but not at all cost.

Win with dignity, lose with grace.

Observe the laws and regulations of the game.

Respect opponents, referees and all participants.

Reject cheating, racism, violence and drugs.

Value volunteers and paid officials alike.

Enjoy the Game.[6]

The following are the core values that the RFU has determined lie at the heart of the game:

1. **Teamwork** – Teamwork is essential to our sport. We welcome all new team members and include all because working as a team enriches our lives. We play selflessly: working for the team, not for ourselves alone, both on and off the field. We take pride in our team, rely on one another and understand that each player has a part to play. We speak out if our team or sport is threatened by inappropriate words or actions.

2. **Respect** – Mutual respect forms the basis of our sport. We hold in high esteem our sport, its values and traditions, and earn the respect of others in the way we behave. We respect our match officials and accept our decisions. We respect opposition players and supporters. We value our coaches and those who run our clubs and treat clubhouses with consideration.

3. **Enjoyment** – Enjoyment is the reason we play and support rugby union. We encourage players to enjoy training and playing. We use our sport to adopt a healthy lifestyle and build life skills. We safeguard our young players and help them have fun. We enjoy being part of a team and part of the rugby family.

4. **Discipline** – Strong discipline underpins our sport. We ensure that our sport is one of controlled physical endeavour and that we are honest and fair. We obey the laws of the game, which ensure an inclusive and exciting global game. We support our disciplinary system, which protects our sport and upholds its values. We observe the sport's laws and regulations and report serious breaches.

5. **Sportsmanship** – Sportsmanship is the foundation upon which rugby union is built. We uphold the rugby tradition of camaraderie with teammates and opposition. We observe fair play both on and off the pitch and are generous in victory and dignified in defeat. We play

to win but not at all costs and recognise both endeavour and achievement. We ensure that the well-being and development of individual players is central to all rugby activity.

Whether or not you live in England, these five core values are a good starting point for discussing a common value system for the sport. Coaches, parents and players all have a role to play in maintaining the right ethos in the game.

Winning is a short-term strategy

Nowhere in RFU's core values will you find any reference to winning as an aim or desirable outcome in age grade rugby.

To the uber competitive individuals out there, the following advice is going to be difficult to accept at first, but we believe that it is essential in order to create successful minis and youth rugby teams.

It is not about the winning.

The principle is simple. Give all players playing time and build a squad with no 'best players'.

This may seem counterintuitive at first and there is certainly good reason to explore this issue as competition can provide an environment in which players improve and push themselves far beyond what they would have achieved had they progressed at their own pace.

However, at minis and youth level it is important to create an environment where all players are valued, regardless of their progress or innate skill, as they change and grow (or not, as the case may be).

The following is the experience of one of our coaches, who has applied this strategy with great success:

'At every game I played every player (we don't do leagues in our part of the world) and while we lost a fair few games, my squad remained mates, all improved their individual skills and continued through youth age groups into Colts[7] with excellent numbers.

While this was happening, some of the bigger clubs who had mini section age groups of 40 or 50 started to pick A and B teams and started to pick teams to win week in and week out. I observed from a distance that some players who trained at every session never got to start in the matches and in some cases never got a game for weeks at a time.

After a while, these players drifted away from training, stopped turning out and sadly seemed to give up the game. These clubs went from 40 to 50 players in an age group to 30 or so as they tried to run two teams. This was then compounded by some of the B team players also wandering off as they were shunned by lads who should have been squad mates and coaches who should have been developing players to the point that they ran one team.

However, this isn't the end of the decline – lads at 16/17 years of age have college, jobs and all the other distractions that come at that age, and sadly this too dents squad numbers, and we get to the point at the start of Colts rugby with these once mighty teams not being able to field a team at all. Roll this on to the numbers of new players joining their senior squads this year and they might have 4 or 5 compared to the 20+ we have welcomed.'

This is, of course, the experience of just one rugby coach, but we have encountered many youth and minis coaches who have observed this same phenomenon.

The same coach continued with this example:

'The club's recent run in the league with their first team would underline the potential for success in this long term approach to player development. The first team for the last season comprised 13 players who were a product of the club's youth and mini teams, they had an average age of 21. During the season they lost one game and defended the regional cup.

The reasons for this? Well, they were a bonded, strong group of players who knew the strengths and weaknesses of their teammates and played to them. Off the pitch they socialised and at training they worked for each other.

At the end of the season not only had they finished league championships (promoting the club to its highest ever league standing), won the regional cup, but they had one of the best home records in the game in the UK.'

For this reason, we propose that a 'win all' approach is a very short-term strategy that may win your team some minis/youth games but can be detrimental to rugby clubs in the long term.

This is not to say that teams should never focus on doing well and winning matches, but there should be a slowly shifting focus towards competition only as the players get older and develop in skill and confidence. This should be done in the following way:

- Beginners – focus on fun and learning through play;
- Minis and Youth – focus on learning to train and training to play; and
- Advanced Youth – focus on training to win and elite player development.

So if your team strategy is not focused on winning, what do you focus on?

Encouraging development

Our focus as coaches for our minis and youth teams should be to develop players to be better next week than they were in the previous week.

Further to this is the understanding that every one of the players in our mini/youth squads should have the potential to play in our seniors squad, and they need to be nurtured and given the opportunity to develop – something that will not happen if they don't get played.

Somewhere in that Under 7s age group is your future club captain – and that player may not necessarily be the best player at the age of seven. However, with the right encouragement, confidence building, training and hard work, that player can develop into a great player over time – and his/her desire to keep playing rugby and improve can be a great inspiration to others.

Not every child will go on to become the next Jonny Wilkinson or Maggie Alphonsi, but that doesn't mean that he/she shouldn't have the opportunity to become the best player he or she can be. Players will take the confidence they gain through playing and being part of a team into other facets of their lives to become more confident people and members of society with a 'can do' attitude.

The effect that rugby can have on the lives of individuals was explored recently in a popular TV series called 'School of Hard Knocks'. The programme used the game of rugby to teach crucial life lessons and core values to troubled and unemployed young men between the ages of 17 and 24, who were serious about undergoing a life-changing experience, to allow them to take forward steps into the world of employment. The show uses the game of rugby to develop confidence and instil a hard work mentality in the participants, which is then translated into real life employment opportunities.[8]

Pedro, the captain of the School of Hard Knocks side in the 2013 series in Glasgow, said that the experience had changed his life and given him the confidence to do things for the first time: 'I [hope] that this game of rugby sets the tone for the rest of our lives. It is possible to change. It is possible to improve ourselves. It is possible to achieve great things.'[9] This is the powerful effect that rugby can have.

It is important to remember that, beyond playing, rugby can teach players the importance of hard work, respect and friendship – qualities that will put players in good stead both on and off the pitch.

Instilling a love of the game

Why do children play any sport? Because it is fun. Rugby coaches need to consider this and make sure that the number one priority is that children have fun playing so that they choose to play the sport and continue to play the game well into their adult years.

Instilling the love of the game and providing players with the opportunity to develop and play the game is the single most important role of a coach. By putting in this effort, coaches are literally investing in the future of their rugby clubs, the future rugby paths (or careers) of their players and the sport as a whole.

Inspiration can be taken from Lindsay Hilton, a female Canadian rugby player who was born without limbs (a quadruple amputee):[10] 'I play rugby because I love the sport – it's very social, it's more a community than anything, so it is a great time.'

Parental support

Parents can share the responsibility of supporting their children's love of playing by becoming active participants in the rugby community. This can range from attending matches to helping support the rugby club by assisting with fundraisers or helping the team with the weekly kit washing. Your involvement will show your child that you support them and their team.

Rugby clubs and coaches should take the opportunity of involving parents in their children's rugby experience. For example, in the summer, pre-season fitness sessions can be opened to every player, mum, dad, etc. It takes a bit of logistical management, but this can further allow parents to get on board with what the coach is trying to accomplish over the course of the season.

A key part of supporting the coach and the ethos that the coach is trying to instil in the team is abiding by the Code of Conduct and staying calm and supportive during rugby matches – even when the referee's calls may not be going the way you want. There is nothing worse than an aggressive parent on the sidelines yelling at their child, the opposition or the referee.

In 2014, a father watching his son's Under 16 team losing heavily in the Hertfordshire Shield Cup Final was caught on camera sticking out his foot and tripping a player on the opposite youth team just as he was about to score a try.[11] The incident caused a huge uproar in the rugby community over respect in rugby and supporters' conduct and led to rugby club campaigns to encourage parents to exercise proper sideline etiquette, including some amusing signs like the following from Bryncoch RFC, aimed at spectators who take matches a bit too seriously:

'Please remember. The players are children. The coaches are volunteers. And the referees do not see everything. This is mini/junior rugby, not the final of the world cup. Enjoy the game and your visit to Bryncoch RFC.'[12]

The sign won a lot of support on social media, with former Wales international Rupert Moon and international rugby referee Nigel Owens, among others, praising it for the excellent reminder to spectators.

Senior player support

In addition to parental support, minis and youth players need consistent support from senior players to excel. This is because youngsters need role models they can look up to, respect and strive to emulate. Youth players also need to see that there are opportunities for them in the senior teams at their club.

It is extremely rewarding to see the adult first teams consisting of players who have progressed through the ranks all the way from mini to youth to the adult teams.

Rugby clubs need to create supportive environments whereby teams of all levels support each other and the senior players attend the minis and youth games when possible to support the future of their rugby clubs (and vice versa).

Senior players should be encouraged to come down on Sunday mornings to coach the minis teams and get involved with the youth sections. This will foster the development of a 'one club/one family' environment where players feel supported and loved and one that players will never want to leave.

The approaches to game play and structures used in the senior squads should be shared with the youth and mini teams and coaches from the minis sections should be able to share ideas and work towards a common goal with the senior coaches.

Youth teams can approach games in exactly the same way as the seniors by, for example, replicating match day warm-ups and routines. This will lead to the youth players understanding that by turning up to train they will be treated seriously and given the best training the club can provide.

Respect, discipline and sportsmanship

Respect and discipline are so fundamental to the ethos of the game of rugby that it is not an exaggeration to say that it differentiates the sport from any other. The difference can perhaps be demonstrated in the experiences of one father who took his seven-year-old son to a birthday party where football was played, with most of the children present aged seven or younger.

His son played Under 7s rugby for the local club where, as well as developing rugby skills, he received a thorough exposure to the RFU's core values of Teamwork, Respect, Enjoyment, Discipline and Sportsmanship. His son usually had little to do with football beyond a passing interest in the sport on TV; however, he seemed to enjoy himself racing around after the ball, putting in the odd tackle, making the odd pass and nicking a goal late in the game. Here is the experience of his father in his own words:

'I had a spare half-hour to kill so I hung around to watch for a while, but after about 15–20 minutes I had to leave. Not because I was pushed for time, but because I couldn't bear to watch the antics of some of the players any longer and was feeling increasingly irritated by the referee's failure to do anything about it.

The worst offender was a seven-year-old who had been scouted by a professional side for their academy and behaved throughout like a cut-down version of Wayne Rooney – face contorted with aggression, flying recklessly into tackles and chasing after retribution following every perceived offence against him.

He also won two free kicks by diving to con the referee, dragged players back by the shirt if they beat him and then laughed after he was eventually penalised, and worst of all (for me at any rate) appealed to the referee at every opportunity, arms outstretched in innocence, including after his own fouls on others.

To cap it all off, he also feigned injury twice – on the second occasion rolling around on the floor in apparent agony so the referee walked over to see him, allowing the game to run unsupervised. Then the ball came near them, at which point the lad jumped up, ran forward with the ball and scored.

Now, I realise that I might sound a bit ranty; point taken. But bear in mind I watched at most 40 per cent of the game and I've described – accurately – the behaviour of just one of the players, and there were several others behaving badly.

My point is this: that player's behaviour wouldn't have been tolerated at our mini rugby sessions; he'd have had the verbal equivalent of a warning, final warning, then yellow card.

'Any attempts to cheat, backchat to coaches, argue with teammates or other disruptive behaviour are met with firm action. If after two warnings a player carries on with their nonsense, they have 5 minutes sitting next to their mum or dad, and a quick chat with parents in attendance before they are allowed to rejoin play.'

When children and their parents are new to rugby, it is a case of educating them in the ethos of sportsmanship that characterises the game at the grass-roots level. It just requires a consistency of approach in dealing with disrespect or bad sportsmanship, and players learn, sooner or later, what they can and cannot get away with. In the vast majority of cases, with the parents' full support, the child starts to toe the line – and as they're no longer being told off all the time, they enjoy their rugby more.

Cheating, gamesmanship, dissent and all other forms of disrespect to the ethos of rugby, especially 'simulation' and appealing for decisions from the referee, should be dealt with firmly in accordance with refereeing guidelines (see page 87–88) and the laws of the game (see page 79–85).

To those who say 'they're only kids', the response should be that this is 'all the more reason to teach them the right way to behave – get them into good habits early'. From talking to parents of children who play team sports, it's clear that one of their concerns is that their children might learn undesirable traits such as cheating or disrespect for authority.

This is the main difference currently between football and rugby: that on the whole, match officials in rugby are more effective at dealing with bad behaviour from players. With the use of technology at the highest levels, things that the officials miss can be referred to a citing panel, and retribution is usually swift. Even at amateur levels, the use of the sin-bin, the ability to take play forward 10 metres for backchat, the option to reverse a penalty for retaliation or other foul play, and even for dissent, are all powerful tools in a rugby referee's armoury that, when used correctly, keep the game true to its ethos of respect and sportsmanship.

And when a referee delivers a lecture, as in Nigel Owens' famous 'This is not soccer' speech to Tobias Botes[13], it usually hits home and behaviour is adjusted.

So if you are a coach or a parent, the next time a referee pings one of your Under 10s players for handing off, don't start heckling from the touchline – this is not soccer, after all.

The vanishing team

What follows is a cautionary tale about how getting your team ethos wrong can have drastic effects on player numbers, driving even the most committed players out of the game. The player drain at our local club is generally minimal; some of the older teams sometimes struggle to field a side, but this is due to the effects of representative and schools rugby (and in September and March/April, the rugby league season) more than any other factor. Only one of our teams has had an issue with players leaving in significant numbers recently that could be attributed to how the team was run, and in our minds it serves as an object lesson in the dangers of getting your ethos wrong.

A new head coach took over the team at Under 12s, and immediately the approach shifted from inclusive to elitist. The team was built around what suited those the coach openly liked to call his 'elite' players (by inference, the rest were the non-elite). Winning games became the only criterion for success, though the coach would deny it, and this was evident from the way the team played, and from which players played the whole of every game and which were always on the bench or subbed at half-time. Training sessions would often consist of one group working on skills with lots of input, with another group aimlessly kicking or passing the ball back and forth with an occasional word or two of encouragement. No prizes for guessing which group the elite players were in!

In matches, certain players would see lots of the ball, while others would only touch it if the opposition kicked it to them. Tries were scored in the main by the same two players; at the end of the season, this was recognised with a trophy for the top try scorer based on a league table published to the whole age group including, at the bottom, those players who never scored because they never got the ball.

Even in terms of behaviour, the coach's indulgence of his elite boys meant that 'weaker' teammates could be bullied and ostracised without consequence, because the coach was afraid of parents taking their boys to another club, thereby affecting results on the pitch. In a game I refereed, I heard one player say to a teammate that 'I won't be coming off because my mum's threatened to take me to a rival RFC if he subs me'.

What this coach failed to see was that what made his players 'elite' at Under 12s and Under 13s was, in the main, their size and speed advantage over their peers.

While this gave them success in terms of match results – at Under 13s they lost only one game, a tournament final – it was a disaster for long-term player development and for the squad as a whole. With the coach focusing his efforts on the elite players, and building the team's game plan around their size and speed, he neglected smaller, slower players – who nonetheless would work extremely hard in training and matches – with the result that these players drifted away. What some of these players also had was excellent game sense and understanding of positional and unit play.

Now at Under 15s, the team loses as many games as it wins, relies on dual-registered rugby league players to fulfil fixtures, has lost one elite player to a rival club because he wanted to be in a winning team – and, most of all, could really do with four or five players whose positional and unit skills, work rate and reading of the game could make the difference between winning and losing tight matches. Even as I write this, the team has reached a crisis point and may even cease to exist if more players leave – though the club has, at last, decided to act by placing the coach under supervision, so with luck the situation will now start to improve. Is the same thing happening in your club, or another you know of?

2 RUGBY FUNDAMENTALS AND HEALTH AND SAFETY

It is the responsibility of coaches and parents to guide young players and teach them the fundamentals of the sport in the right way at an early age.

In the UK, minis and youth rugby can be taught to girls and boys together until the age of 12 and is split by gender thereafter. If a child is under the age of 12, it will be important to consider whether a mixed-gender team is right for them or whether a single-sex group is better.

There has been evidence to demonstrate that girls benefit from playing together with boys at an early age and certainly many professional women players who have played from a very young age in mixed teams will testify to this. However, according to the Irish Rugby Football Union, 'most rugby clubs encourage girls to join mixed minis rugby but research has shown that when separate "boy" and "girl" sections are available, more girls participate and continue to play and enjoy the game.'[14]

Regardless of whether a child is involved in a mixed-gender group or not, there are many health and safety issues to consider for coaches and parents.

Height, size and skill

Children grow at different speeds, so it is not surprising that there will be a discrepancy in the heights and sizes of children playing rugby in the same age groups. It is also not surprising that some children pick up sporting skills faster than others.

This is contributed by the fact that children born in the earlier months of the year have a clear advantage over those born in the later months. In *Superfreakonomics*, Steven D. Levitt and Stephen J. Dubner revealed that 43 per cent of European soccer players were born in the first three months of the year, while only 9 per cent were born in the last three months of the year. According to the book, 'Children who are a few months older than their peers at 5 or 6 have more developed cognitive and motor skills, which makes them more advanced athletes and students. This early advantage can lead to self-fulfilling prophecies later on: the child thinks she is an underachiever, and so will often play that role.'[15]

In a contact sport like rugby, size may be of greater importance than in other sports once players transition into the contact aspect of the game, which in England occurs when children reach the age of nine, with a staged progression into full contact. This will be discussed in more depth in Chapter 6.

For this reason, it is important to make sure that the ethos of rugby remains focused on development and instilling the love of the game in players, rather than on winning. This will allow younger and smaller players to continue to enjoy playing rugby and not feel threatened by their slower development in size or skill. After a few years these younger or smaller players may end up being the best players on the team.

This can be exemplified by the legendary Brian O'Driscoll, an Irish International and British Lion who retired from rugby in 2014. The following is an excerpt from the *Irish Examiner*:

> 'O'Driscoll was small for his age but hugely skilful and hugely determined. What particularly struck McGinty was how O'Driscoll refused to play the victim.
>
> "When fellas that are good footballers don't get on a team you can get histrionics but Brian just got on with it. In fact at the end of that cup campaign I would get a lovely letter from Brian's father, Frank, saying how much Brian enjoyed the season and being part of that squad.
>
> "And if you look through Brian's career, he's maintained that attitude. He's shown huge perseverance and taken every setback in his stride, whether it was losing a game to win a Grand Slam or lasting only a couple of minutes as the [2005] Lions captain or not making the final Test team on his last Lions tour he's always maintained his poise and dignity. And I think a lot of that comes from his parenting."'[16]

O'Driscoll's rugby ethos – his focus on development, determination to improve and love for the game – led him to become one of the best and most loved players in the world. We as parents and coaches should try to encourage players to emulate this attitude and promote it by giving players the opportunity to play and improve as they grow.

Macho culture

It is important that as parents and coaches we do not promote physicality at the expense of technique as this can be very damaging to younger players and the sport as a whole. While we all can enjoy a big 'hit' when watching international rugby, we need to be mindful that we do not encourage children to emulate this behaviour when they do not possess the proper form, technique, training and physique to sustain this kind of physicality.

We have heard coaches encourage players as young as nine and ten to put in 'big hits' – and not always legally.

One of our coaches writes:

'I've had to speak to the forwards in an U11 game when as they packed down for the first scrum, the visiting hooker was exhorting his colleagues to put in a "massive hit lads, let's smash 'em off the park". I hear coaches calling out to key players to make "dominant" tackles and to "dump him backwards" and have had to warn players about potentially dangerous tackles even in U10 rugby.

In an U12 game a player was tackled round the neck as he attempted to score, and not only was the perpetrator not penalised (bad refereeing), but he was clapped on the back by teammates and cheered by parents and coaches for a "great hit" (as opposed to being picked up for incorrect and dangerous tackling technique).

In a recent conversation with an orthopaedic consultant, I was told that the limb and joint injuries he now sees in rugby players are similar to injuries he sees in motor-cyclists hit by cars. This was when we were discussing a player's torn anterior cruciate ligament (ACL), picked up at the age of 11, through being hit ridiculously hard from the side while his studs were caught in the ground.

There was nothing illegal about the tackle, and the injury was down to bad luck as much as any other factor, but the tackler had stepped over the line from committed (which is desirable in a tackle) to "hard". The end result is that after a partial recovery, he has had to give up the game at the age of 13 and will need an operation once he stops growing, after which he may or may not play again.'

So the message to coaches and parents is that while commitment in contact is essential, excessive aggression is not. Children, especially teenage boys, are naturally aggressive and do not need to be encouraged to be more aggressive.

Junior coaches and referees have a duty of care to all players, not just their own, and need to remember that the players being smashed don't necessarily have the strength and conditioning to withstand huge impacts.

With the very youngest players, or with anyone new to the game, we also need to consider the emotional impact of being on the end of a huge hit. Even if there is no physical injury, being unceremoniously clattered by someone bigger, heavier and nastier than you can induce feelings of fear and humiliation, neither of which is conducive to enjoyment of the game. This will only be made worse if they then hear howls of approbation from the opposition coaches and parents on the touchline.

The young players in our care are generally playing for enjoyment and to be part of a team, not with any serious ambitions to play top-flight rugby, so there's no need to try to produce miniature internationals.

Those who are good enough to be picked up through the representative system will develop a harder edge to their play through having to compete at a higher standard, and this will benefit them and their club/school sides. For the less developed players, who aren't able to give the same level of physical commitment, we risk ruining the experience of rugby for them if we set expectations for all the team to tackle hard and be physically aggressive and dominant.

Please remember that the safety and well-being of all players comes before the satisfaction of seeing a big hit. If we promote good technique in the tackle, scrum and other contact phases of the game, rather than looking for the big hit, we'll have a safer, happier game for all participants.

Concussion

'Concussion is singularly the most important topic in rugby at the moment,' said James Robson, Scotland's doctor in more than a hundred Tests and six-time Chief Medical Officer for the British & Irish Lions.[17]

A concussion is a temporary injury to the brain that can be sustained by players through impact – blows to the head, face or neck, or a blow to the body that causes a sudden jarring of the head.

Studies have shown that concussions occur in one in every 21 games played by an amateur adult rugby player. There are no statistics available for age grade rugby, but it is reasonable to assume that these figures would be lower than this.

Coaches have the most important role in the prevention and management of player concussion during training and rugby matches and all coaches should be able to recognise suspected concussion as they are in the best position to remove a player who has suffered from concussion from play.

If in doubt, it is our recommendation that a player showing any signs or symptoms of concussion should be removed from the pitch and not be allowed back to continue playing. Furthermore, players who have suffered concussion in the past must be treated with even greater scrutiny and not be allowed back to play until the recommended stand-down period for the player's age and level of concussion is met.

All RFU Licensed Coaches must now take a mandatory player safety course to assist them with their understanding of concussion. This is especially important for youth coaches because young players are often unfamiliar with the symptoms of concussion and may not know or admit to having sustained one.

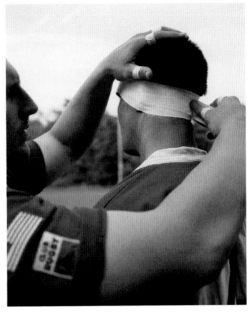

Concussion is more than a visible issue

According to the RFU, research also shows that young players in particular rely on their coach to provide information about concussion and are influenced most in their attitude towards concussion by their coach.[18]

Concussion and player safety information is built into the RFU's coach, referee and medical education programmes as part of the 'Don't be a Headcase' programme, and the HEADCASE online resource developed with the Headway charity has been praised as the leading resource in sport in the UK. The quality of the RFU's resources has been endorsed by Dr Richard Greenwood, a Consultant Neurologist at Homerton Hospital and the National Hospital for Neurology and Neurosurgery, who said: 'Having reviewed the RFU's HEADCASE resource as an independent expert, I think that it is an excellent source of information for those involved with rugby. It is an accurate, thorough and appropriate source of information, based on the most up to date medical consensus. The RFU should be applauded for making this available in such an accessible format.'

The RFU has put in place new standards relating to the management of concussion and extending the reach of its concussion education initiatives. The return to play pathway for players who have sustained a concussion is dependent on the player's age and the medical resources they can access. The new routine minimum stand-down period is 23 days for Under 19s.

The minimum stand-down period for those in an Enhanced Care Setting – typically professional and elite age-group players – is 12 days for Under 17–19s. These are players whose return to play pathway is closely supervised by an appropriately trained and suitably experienced medical practitioner.

World Rugby acknowledges the diversity in health care support available in different countries and at different levels, and permits member unions to adapt similar guidelines to those adopted by the RFU to suit their local circumstances.

These stand-down periods are to be seen as the minimum periods before a player can return to play and may be longer where appropriate. The return to play pathway is made up of rest and Graduated Return To Play (GRTP) phases. The length of these phases for an individual is determined by the player's recovery and informed by clinical assessment.

The measures have been approved by the Professional Game Board and the Community Game Board, the two bodies that manage the game in England.

Dr Mike England, the RFU Community Rugby Medical Director, said: 'We hope everyone involved in the game – parents, players, coaches and medics – takes the rationale for the changes on board and finds it helpful in managing concussion in conjunction with the online HEADCASE resources the RFU provides and the guidance we've made widely available to the game through coaching, refereeing and medical education.

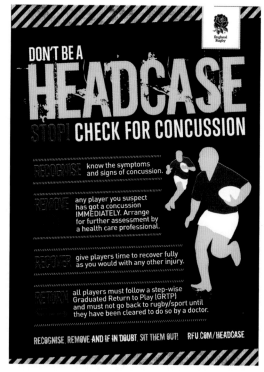

Expert advice is that concussion should be managed on an individual basis. There is a need however for more clarity and guidance to reinforce the message that players need time to recover fully before returning to play and that young players in particular need to be managed more conservatively than adults. What hasn't changed is that being able to return to play is still a clinical decision based on an individual player's recovery.'

Image used with kind permission of the RFU. The RFU Rose and the words 'England Rugby' are official registered trade marks of the Rugby Football Union

More information can be found at: www.rfu.com/headcase

Like the RFU, many countries are combating the dangers of concussion in different ways. In 49 of the 50 United States, this risk is being addressed through the legislative process by requiring parents, players and coaches to undergo concussion education as part of the Lystedt law.

Stretching

Stretching is an important aspect of injury prevention and should be taught to players from a very early age. We recommend dynamic stretching before a training session or match and static stretching at the end of a session or match.

The difference between dynamic and static stretching is movement. Dynamic stretching involves moving a joint or muscle through a series of repetitive motions with the aim of extending the movement with every repetition. Examples of dynamic stretching include walking lunges, walking kicks and walking hamstring stretches. The key is movement, which is designed to help prepare the body for the upcoming exercise and reduce the likelihood of injury.

Static stretches aim to increase flexibility by relaxing the body into the stretch in a static position (without movement). Examples of static stretches include standing hamstring stretch, butterfly adductor stretch, sitting bent knee hamstring stretch, lying down gluteal stretch, etc. Static stretches involve holding the stretch for 30–60 seconds in a challenging position to increase flexibility.

PRE-EXERCISE STRETCHING

According to sporting performance analyst and FRN blogger Liz Ward, unless a player's performance is gymnastic or balletic, static stretching before a session is not necessary and is unlikely to prevent injury, so it is more important for players and coaches to set aside time to perform a full range of dynamic stretching, which will provide functional preparation for the players before playing rugby.

A thorough warm-up is vitally important in reducing the incidence of injury because muscles need to be warmed and the synovial fluid needs to get flowing.

Start getting players familiar with dynamic flexibility stretches, which will help them maintain and improve their flexibility as they age.

Dynamic stretching will not only give the muscles and joints the attention they need prior to physical activity but warming up in this way also gives the cardiovascular system a chance to get into gear. Getting the heart rate going as you stretch with a gradual increase of intensity helps the body ease into exercise. We therefore recommend that players be guided from simpler dynamic stretches into more difficult ones, ending with sprints at 25, 50 and 100 per cent.

The most important thing to remember when stretching is that if you cannot FEEL THE STRETCH, you can be sure you are not GETTING THE STRETCH. Players need to play around with different movements and positions until they can feel that they are stretching the right muscle. Obviously this is more difficult for younger players to do, so coaches will need to carefully supervise stretching sessions and invest time for stretching in training and game-day sessions.

Make sure players stretch both BEFORE and AFTER training sessions and matches. This will encourage them to form good habits while they are young, which will keep them fit and healthy well into their playing years.

Here are ten dynamic stretches every player should perform before the start of a session:

- Walking on toes (A)
- Walking hamstring stretch (leg in front) (B)
- Walking hamstring stretch (leg behind)
- Walking lunges
- Walking squats (C)
- Walking kicks (D)
- Carioca (E & F)
- Jumps (knee bent) (G)
- Back kicks (H)
- High knees (I)

POST-EXERCISE STRETCHING

Post-exercise stretching is also a key factor in avoiding injury and should not be ignored. When players train or play, their muscles work really hard contracting and stretching to allow them to move. By the end of the activity, the muscles have shortened and need to be stretched. Importantly, therefore, they need to be stretched when still warm – before players leave the arena, whether it be a rugby pitch, sports field, tennis court or any other sporting environment.

If players do not stretch their muscles at this time, they cool down shortened, which means that players start their next activity with shortened muscles. Stretching while the muscles are still warm means that they cool down lengthened and stay lengthened until the next training session or match.

Here are ten static stretches every player should perform after the start of a session:

- Triceps stretch (A)
- Supraspinatus stretch (front of arm) (B)
- Head stretches (forward, back, apply force)
- Quadriceps stretch (C)
- Hamstring stretch with knee bent (D)
- Standing hamstring stretch (E)
- Abductor stretch (F)
- Gluteal stretch
- Lumbar rotation stretch
- Gluteal and lumbar rotation stretch
- Hip flexor stretch

A

B

C

D

E

F

Disability in rugby

Rugby is an inclusive game – it has a role for everyone regardless of factors such as shape, size or fitness level. As coaches, we've strived to make the teams we look after in the youth and minis understand it's the team that matters, not the individuals within it. This is an opportunity to interact with a wider demographic than the young players encounter in their schools.

As an example, we were approached while promoting the club at an activity fair by a 13-year-old girl who wanted to join our girls' team. Obviously we welcomed her with open arms. Her comment to her mother – 'You promised if they had a girls' team I could go' – was good enough for us.

The girl had been removed from school by her mother after the school excluded her from playing sport. She suffered from cerebral palsy and at the time her motor skills were affected but she really wanted to play. The team made her welcome at training and she played numerous games with us.

As coaches, this story gives us a sense of pride in the club, the game and its players. Here was a young girl excluded from school through no fault of her own, with a very small social circle at age 13, who suddenly had a group of mates. A group of mates who involved her off the pitch as much as on it, who took her shopping, and still to this day keep in regular contact. As for her motor skills, they improved in time playing rugby, and she stopped using a wheelchair when out shopping with the team. She was just one of the team. No special consideration, just included.

WHEELCHAIR RUGBY

Rugby also offers a version to wheelchair users. There is a variety of wheelchair rugby options, including Wheelchair Rugby Union, Wheelchair Rugby League and Wheelchair Rugby Sevens, and some varieties are open to both disabled and fully abled players, which provides a great opportunity for family and friends to play with wheelchair-users.

Wheelchair Rugby is a full contact game and is played on basketball courts. It formed the basis of a film called *Murderball*, which follows the US wheelchair rugby team during a season. It is an inspirational film and well worth a watch.

The game has a number of teams in the UK and around the world and, as with any rugby club, anywhere will welcome new players.

Player safety

Like any other contact sport, rugby poses a risk of injury to players.

At professional level, rugby has continually demanded more and more physicality and size from players. In fact, World Rugby has reported that between 2000 and 2015 there has been on average a 10 per cent increase in player weight across positions in international rugby. In this same period, the average number of tackles per match has risen from 160 to 220.

At the same time, players are still expected to maintain great speed. This is reflected in a 5 per cent drop in the average time for the 10m sprint over the same 15-year period. It is clear from these figures that on a professional level players are expected to be bigger, faster and more skilled than ever before – and this expectation filters down into the amateur game as well.

Amateur teams and players mirror what they see in the professional game, so it is more important than ever that coaches and parents do everything they can to make sure players are safe. Amateur teams and players do not have the same medical support and expertise available to them as the professionals, and younger players' brains are more vulnerable to damage than adults'. However, with the right coaching, the commitment of parents, coaches and players, and a firm dedication to the best interests of players relating to concussion, rugby is a safe game. In fact, other sports, such as American football, have looked to rugby as an example of good technique in relation to contact.

It is therefore more important than ever that we as coaches, parents and supporters look out for our players' health and safety by following the advice in this chapter relating to concussion and stretching and by teaching proper tackling form to players (see Chapter 10).

3 GETTING STARTED

Getting a child involved in rugby is easy. Rugby clubs/teams are usually very friendly and, unlike sports such as cricket, American football or lacrosse, rugby requires little specialised/expensive equipment to get started.

If you are a parent who is interested in supporting your child's interest in rugby, this book will equip you with all the information you need to become familiar with the game and allow you to feel comfortable chatting to other parents and coaches.

In fact, you may find yourself more engaged and educated in age grade rugby than the coach – who is sometimes just a parent volunteer!

Finding the right club

The first thing a child will need to get started is a rugby club that has a minis or youth rugby section. If you live within England, you can find local rugby clubs using the FindRugbyNow website (www.findrugbynow.com) or the RFU portal. Other countries may have similar websites to help you.

It is advisable to call or email the coach in advance to let him know that your child is interested in attending a session and obtain the correct information about practice times. Websites are not always up to date and there is nothing worse than showing up with your child for their first session only to discover that the sessions were moved to another day the previous week.

To keep travel time to a minimum, it is sensible to find a rugby club nearby – your child may be starting a lifetime commitment to the club if he or she chooses to play into adulthood. That said, if you have access to several clubs in your area, it is advisable to visit them all to see which is right for you and your child.

When choosing a rugby club, you will need to consider the following factors:

- History – an older club will usually have a stronger rugby community and a proven track record of success.
- Coaching – have a look at the club's coaching across the age levels and adult teams (your child's coach may be great this year but if his coach the following year isn't, this will affect his ability to progress as a player).
- Ethos – does the club's and the coach's ethos and approach to minis and youth rugby fit with the rugby ethos outlined in Chapter 1? Do players treat coaches and referees with respect? If not, the club may not be right for you and your child.
- Community – does the club have a strong rugby community? Are adult players supportive of youth players? Are second-team players treated with respect?
- Culture – this is different to rugby ethos. Is it a rugby club that drinks or a drinking club that plays rugby? Does the rugby club set the right tone? Do you enjoy speaking with the other club members? You may be spending a lot of time at this club, so this is important.
- RFU Approval – many English clubs now carry the RFU's Community Rugby Seal of Approval, a kind of quality mark for age grade rugby provision. While it doesn't guarantee that everything is perfect at a club, it is a good indicator that things are being done the right way.

If you do not live in the UK, New Zealand, France, Australia, South Africa, or other large rugby-focused country, you may struggle to find a 'rugby club' in the manner described above. Many of the non-traditional rugby nations, like the United States, do not have a history of rugby clubs. Within these countries you may find adult rugby teams without affiliations to a rugby club, so there are fewer development opportunities for mini and youth rugby players. The best place to start is your country's rugby union; however, if no club search is available on their website, try browsing the internet for teams near you.

Clothing and gear

Players will need the following items of rugby kit and gear:

MANDATORY
- Jersey, shorts
- Boots (and socks)

OPTIONAL
- Gumshield (strongly recommended!)
- Scrum cap
- Shoulder pads
- Rugby gloves
- Shin guards
- Chest pad (females only)
- Leggings

Water bottles are also a necessity

We will discuss each of these items below, but please note that this section covers clothing and gear that is currently permissible. Rules can change over time, so make sure you stay up to date with laws and regulations pertaining to your age level and gender.

If you are just learning about the game, you may be surprised to find that rugby players are not provided with a lot of protective gear.

The list of acceptable and unacceptable items is provided in section 4 of the 2012 World Rugby (IRB) laws. The main reason for most of the items on the unacceptable list is player safety. Law 4.4(c) states:

'A player must not wear any items containing buckles, clips, rings, hinges, zippers, screws, bolts or rigid material or projection not otherwise permitted under this Law.'

These items could cause serious injury to the opposition and a player who is caught on the pitch wearing one of these items may be asked to remove it. The World Rugby website states:

'The referee has power to decide at any time, before or during the match, that part of a player's clothing is dangerous or illegal. If the referee decides that clothing is dangerous or illegal the referee must order the player to remove it. The player must not take part in the match until the items of clothing are removed. If, at an inspection before the match, the referee or a touch judge tells a player that an item banned under this Law is being worn, and the player is subsequently found to be wearing that item on the playing area, that player is sent off for misconduct. A penalty kick is awarded at the place where play is restarted.'

This means that before a match, players must take care to remove all jewellery and accessories, including all watches, earrings, wristbands, jewellery and all piercings (regardless of material).

In circumstances where such items cannot be removed (e.g. if a player has only just got his/her ears pierced and is not able to remove the earrings), it is sometimes possible to cover the item with tape to prevent it from injuring to self and others – however, officially all piercings must be removed, so this is at the discretion of the referee.

MANDATORY KIT AND GEAR
Clothing (also known as 'stash' or 'kit')

The standard set of clothing required to play rugby is a jersey, shorts (and socks). Prices for these vary depending on quality and brand. Some of our favourite high-quality brands are Canterbury, Gilbert and Samurai.

In regard to kit-changing, World Rugby laws state that 'a referee must not allow any player to leave the playing area to change items of clothing, unless these are bloodstained'. So, players must make sure they wear the right kit from the start.

The type of jersey and the material of the kit vary depending on the type of rugby being played. Rugby 7s has traditionally opted for very tight figure-hugging kit while 15s rugby preferred a looser fit. However, over time, sublimation kit has become the kit of choice for most national teams in both varieties of rugby, including in Scotland, England and Wales.

A good tight set of kit provides less opportunity for the opponents to grab players speeding away. If you are interested in some bespoke sublimation kit, check out the brands mentioned above.

There is little World Rugby guidance on rugby shorts except that 'a player must not wear shorts with padding sewn into them … or any item that is normally permitted by Law, but, in the referee's opinion that is liable to cause injury to a player'. Choose shorts that fit well and allow the player to move easily while running and kicking. Shorts with a bit of elastic on the waist and crotch area promote comfort of movement.

Although socks are not essential, they are very helpful to protect players from scratches, bruises and grass burns. Modern socks are made using the latest technology to keep them firmly in place on the calves, which avoids the need for taping or fastening, or constantly pulling them up!

Boots

There are several rules regarding which footwear rugby players can wear. The best kind of boots provide players with a good grip on the turf, but are also light enough to allow the players to run quickly throughout the match. Depending on your position on the pitch, you will need to strike a certain balance between these two requirements.

Whichever boots you choose, player safety must be taken into account and the studs on players' boots must abide by the 'Safety Aspects of Rugby Boot Sole Design' set out in Appendix 2 of the World Rugby laws.

Rugby boots suitable for soft ground

Rugby boot studs worn by players 'must not be longer than 21mm, and must not have any burring or sharp edges'. The reason for this restriction is that sharp edges could seriously injure other players during scrums, tackling and especially rucks and collapsed mauls.

Any player would testify that even normal studs can leave nasty marks during the normal course of rugby through glancing, tackling and stamping. It is for this reason that the referee will call a stud check before the start of any match to ensure that the players are wearing appropriate boots. Moulded rubber multi-studded soles are acceptable provided they have no sharp edges or ridges.

The equipment players wear can protect from injuries, but unauthorised equipment can get them sent off – so make sure they stay safe and injury-free and wear the right gear.

The World Rugby Specifications, which include the provisions relating to players' dress (Regulation 12), can be found on the World Rugby website here: http://laws.worldrugby.org/index.php?law=4

Gumshield

Undoubtedly the most important protection that a rugby player can wear is a gumshield (also known as a mouthguard). The gumshield not only protects the player's teeth and gums, but it can reduce damage to the jaw and reduces a player's chances of getting concussed.

The gumshield has evolved and progressed over time and now the best thing a player can do for protection is to order a custom gumshield. One of our favourite brands of custom gumshields is Opro, for quality and convenience. Trays can be sent to your home address, and can be fitted in just a few minutes without a trip to the dentist.

A well fitted gumshield is necessary

Most importantly, custom gumshields offer a better level of protection, but also comfort – and mouthy scrum halves can enjoy a gumshield that stays put in action.

You can find more information about gumshields and the benefits of custom gumshields here: http://findrugbynow.com/2012/03/the-1-protection-against-injury/.

At the time of publication, gumshields are not mandatory for boys and men's rugby but are mandatory for girls' youth age groups. Regardless of the legality, we believe that gumshields are crucial for players and both parents and coaches should require their use by players at ANY level.

OPTIONAL KIT AND GEAR
Scrum cap
The scrum cap adds an extra layer of protection and is often used by forwards to protect their heads from scrum impact and also to protect their ears when they are bound. However, some backs, especially centres that often go into contact, also opt to wear a scrum cap.

Modern scrum caps are made from cell foam padding and include a chin strap to ensure maximum protection and comfort (and that the cap does not come flying off during the match). The cap should fit the head tightly yet comfortably.

Players with a history of concussion may choose to wear scrum caps as an added layer of protection, but these caps are not helmets and are not designed to completely prevent the impact as they are soft and thin.

The World Rugby law states that: 'A player may wear headgear made of soft and thin materials provided that no part of the headgear is thicker than 1cm when uncompressed and no part of the headgear has a density of more than 45kg per cubic metre.'
Some players prefer not to wear scrum caps because they can diminish hearing, which can impact their game. And some players just don't like the way they look in scrum caps!

There are many brands of scrum cap, including Gilbert (http://www.gilbertrugby.com), Canterbury (http://www.canterbury.com) and Optimum (http://optimumsport.com), which range in price. If you are interested in buying one for a player, try out several brands to find the one that fits the player best. Remember that the scrum cap must bear the World Rugby Approval Mark (Regulation 12).

Shoulder pads

The World Rugby rules state that players may wear shoulder pads 'made of soft and thin materials, which may be incorporated in an undergarment or jersey provided that the pads cover the shoulder and collar-bone only. No part of the pads may be thicker than 1cm when uncompressed. No part of the pads may have a density of more than 45kg per cubic metre.'

Like shin guards (discussed below), it is not mandatory for players to wear shoulder pads and sometimes it is not the practice in amateur sides, although in women's rugby these have sometimes been combined with chest pads to create a good addition to women's kit.

If you want to try out some shoulder pads, remember that the pads must bear the World Rugby Approval Mark (Regulation 12).

Rugby gloves

In winter or in difficult conditions, players can also opt to wear rugby gloves. These not only help to keep the players' hands warm on a cold day but also provide players with a better grip on the ball.

There is a debate as to whether wearing rugby gloves actually improves a player's control and handling of the ball, but some players swear by them, so it is worth giving them a try to see if they work for you.

Gloves are fingerless, which allows the player to get a good grip on the ball. The palms of the gloves should also include special ridges and sticky material to keep the ball from falling out of the player's hands (sometimes called 'super grip palm').

If you are thinking of making your own rugby gloves instead of buying some, be careful. The World Rugby rules state that 'Coverage of the fingers and thumbs [is] permitted to the outer joint but no further. The mitt zone of coverage should not continue beyond the wrist. The body of the mitt should be of a stretch type material with the grip material being made of a soft rubber/synthetic compound not exceeding a depth of 1mm.' Also, no part of the mitt can have buttons or potentially dangerous items. So perhaps it is best to leave this one to the pros and buy a pair if you want to try these out. There are many brands of rugby gloves, including Optimum, Canterbury, Gilbert and Kooga. Check out some of the cool designs and patterns or get patriotic and wear your country's team colours.

Shin guards

According to the World Rugby rules, a player may wear shin guards under his/her socks 'with padding incorporated in non-rigid fabric with no part of the padding thicker than 0.5cm when compressed'.

Shin guards are allowed in rugby and they certainly do add a layer of protection to a very vulnerable area of the body. That said, it is our experience that it is unusual for children or adult players at an amateur level to wear shin guards.

If you wish your child to use shin guards, please make sure these conform to the RFU rules and include soft padding. These differ from shin guards used in football.

Chest pads (females only)

The World Rugby laws provide only one difference for the genders in terms of equipment:

'Besides the previous items, women may wear chest pads made of soft and thin materials which may be incorporated as part of a garment provided that the pads cover the shoulder and/or collar-bone and/or chest only with no part of the pads thicker than 1cm when uncompressed and no part of the pads having a density of more than 45kg per cubic metre.'

The pads must also bear the World Rugby Approval Mark (Regulation 12).

Women at an amateur level seldom wear chest pads as these tend to be expensive, bulky and unnecessary. However, in recent years there have been some good strides in combining chest pads with shoulder pads (see page 41), which World Rugby have approved.

Leggings

The law in regard to leggings is that neither adults nor youths under the age of 18 are allowed to wear them. However, there is an exception for youths if it is very cold and the referee deems it appropriate to wear them.

There is an argument to be made that leggings are not a disruption to play and should be allowed, especially for younger children; however, the World Rugby policy is clear. No wearing of leggings unless this is allowed by the referee due to unusually cold conditions.

Player wearing leggings under shorts

RELIGIOUS EXCEPTIONS

Rugby unions have made exceptions for players who are required to wear certain items of clothing on the grounds of religion. This includes allowing women to wear leggings/trousers and head scarves – for example, World Rugby permits the Iranian National 7s team to wear the full body covering that meets the religious rules set down by the rulers of Iran in 2012.

The captain of the Iranian Women's Rugby 7s team, Zohre Eyni, has said: 'The whole team has learnt how to keep the veil in place so that it doesn't interfere with play and I think we have shown that even a physical game like rugby can be played in a veil.'

If a child requires additional exceptions to be made for their religious beliefs, enquire with the coach and World Rugby whether the sport can meet their needs.

4 FOCUS ON PLAYERS

'It's our game, not yours'

The title above is taken from the name of a recent NSPCC campaign in the UK. Devised by the Society's Child Protection in Sport Unit (CPSU), 'It's our game, not yours' seeks to educate adults in how to be good coaches, parents and spectators for their sporting offspring.

It is perhaps a sad indictment on British society that an eminent body like the NSPCC would need to run this type of campaign. However, this is how things are at many junior sports grounds, and it is time the issue was addressed. When parents overstep the mark with their 'encouragement', it can be very damaging, especially because children – unlike professional sportsmen – have no training in how to shut out the crowd. At junior sport, every shout from the touchline is heard on the pitch.

The CPSU's initiative is therefore welcome and, to our minds, hugely effective. Its key tactic is to use actual quotes from children, to highlight their experiences of the bear-pit atmosphere in junior sport and especially to bring it home to adults how this makes them feel. The resources provided for clubs include toolkits on promoting desirable behaviour from parents, challenging inappropriate behaviour, and helping players to raise concerns. It's to be hoped that with persistent application of these principles across junior sports, we can find a way to hand the game back to the players.

All the above serves to introduce this topic: what we (adults involved in age grade rugby) can do to ensure that the focus stays on the players, and that it remains their game, not ours. Everyone who reads this book, if they've ever stood on a touchline at an age grade rugby match, will know that general crowd noise can get pretty loud. Even Under 9s games experience this. Some supporters get quite intensely involved in the game, bellowing instructions at youngsters and criticism at the referee and sometimes even getting a little heated. Is this a wholesome atmosphere to play in, conducive to the child enjoying the experience?

If only it were limited to shouting … Alas, in recent years there have been assaults on referees at junior rugby games in England and Scotland, and even a player tripped by an opposition spectator to prevent him running clear (see page 14). In short, rugby crowds don't always behave as they should.

Beware of your influence

There are also individual parents who harass their own children (and sometimes other people's), shouting criticism for every error, constantly telling them where to stand, who to pass to, what to do next. This incessant and ever-changing stream of instructions – sometimes in contradiction of what the coach is telling the players – is intimidating and confusing to most youngsters. Although it's conceived with good intentions, because the adult wants to help, the advice actually achieves the opposite because of how it is delivered.

Even prior to the start of play, parents can do damage and sap their child's enjoyment of the game. On the way to rugby in the morning, some parents (often the dads) like to wind their children up to get 'in the zone'.

One child in a squad we've coached is a totally different player depending on whether his father brings him to rugby or his mother.

If it's his father, then Jack is a barely controllable ball of aggression on the pitch, almost exploding with frustration whenever a teammate lets him down (i.e. doesn't pass to him), and off the pitch is a barrack-room lawyer, bossy to teammates and argumentative with coaches.

When his mother brings him, Jack still has the fire in the belly but has the ice in the mind to go with it, controls his frustration better and co-operates with teammates and coaches much more readily. Same child, different parent; surely no coincidence? It'd be interesting to have a webcam in his father's car on a Sunday morning!

The journey home can be equally dispiriting for the child, as the session or match is picked apart play by play and suitable homilies delivered on what was done wrong and how you have to try harder next time. Dave Beal used to do this himself, until one day when his son, then aged seven, asked him simply: 'Didn't I do anything good?'

'Of course, he'd done lots of good things, but I was focusing on correcting what he'd done wrong rather than what he'd done well or even more importantly, had he had fun? I'm happy to say, I started to change from that day onward; now, though my son no longer plays due to injury, his younger brother does and we hardly talk at all on the way home, other than to say that I've enjoyed watching him play and having a good time in the clubhouse with his mates. After that, the conversation turns to what he might have for second lunch!'

What all these examples and anecdotes have in common is this: that in each case, the parent has forgotten who this activity is for. These are all classic examples of controlling, egotistical behaviour by adults towards children that turns the child's activity (and their proficiency in pursuing it) into an extension of the adult's sense of self. In other words, it becomes the adult's game, not the child's.

You don't need to be a psychologist to work this out, which is good, because we're not either! So how do we know? We were once children ourselves, and have some experience of this phenomenon.

David's father was a committed sportsman and captain of his school swimming team as well as a keen football and rugby player. Here, David relates an anecdote from his own days as a talented middle-distance runner.

'At 16, Dad was selected to swim for his county team and could have gone on to greater things still, had he not contracted a serious illness and been unable to compete. Thirty years later, when I started to take track athletics seriously and to make some serious improvements to my 800 and 1500m times, Dad would sometimes come and watch. On one memorable occasion, as I sat ninth in a county 1500m final some 50m back from an elite group that had broken away, he shouted encouragement to me: "Get a move on, you're running like a girl!".

'I finished fifth in the end, winning the "race within a race" and more importantly knocking 19 seconds off my personal best, but for a long time all I could remember was dad's "advice". That and the fact that as I hadn't won, despite the quality of the opposition, my best ever performance to date was worthless. Only years later, and discussing similar experiences with my older brother, did I arrive at the conclusion that dad was only trying to help, in a somewhat misguided way. His frustrated sporting ambitions meant he was all the more anxious for his sons to do well, to fulfil our potential, and it got the better of him on that occasion.'

This is how we know where parents are coming from when get too carried away with misguided advice. It won't always be due to frustrated sporting aspirations, but very often just a thrusting, competitive desire to see their child excel (especially in comparison to other people's children).

Most inappropriate parental behaviour at age grade rugby comes not from not knowing how to behave, or lack of understanding of sportsmanship, but from this transference of the parent's desire for success on to their child. Their inner control freak takes over and rather than just letting their child get on and enjoy it, they hector, cajole, advise and even threaten or bully to get the result they want. They justify this by saying they are trying to help their child enjoy the experience and only want what's best for them, but the point is, they want the adult's version of what's best, not the child's.

Child's point of view

Anything that makes parents think about the experience from the child's point of view, encouraging them to let the child enjoy it on their own terms, is to be welcomed with open arms. In age grade rugby, great steps have been taken recently to drive this idea forward and the groundswell of opinion in favour is steadily growing. One obvious example is the way rugby has embraced regulatory and procedural requirements aimed at protecting children from abuse.

All coaches submit to a mandatory Disclosure and Barring Service (DBS) check (formerly known as the Criminal Records Bureau or CRB check) to confirm they have no criminal convictions that should exclude them from working with children, which is renewed every three years.

All players now have to be registered on a national player database and are issued with a photo ID card which confirms that the player is cleared to take part in rugby.

Adult volunteers regularly attend child protection workshops, first aid courses and are even trained in the use of paediatric defibrillators, which can now be found at many clubs. Awareness of particular medical issues, notably the risk of concussion and 'second impact' brain injury in particular, leads to revision of procedures to deal with such incidents more effectively, thereby reducing the risk of serious consequences for young players.[19] All these measures combine to take care of the child's physical welfare, protecting them from injury or abuse.

Great contest for the ball

In looking after children's emotional needs, rugby has been on the ball for some time now. From 2005 (and possibly prior to that) the RFU started to issue a series of Codes of Conduct for coaches, players, parents and spectators. These could have been written with the CPSU's current campaign in mind. They try to encourage the sort of behaviours that will promote the game as being for the players first and foremost (and indeed since 2013 they have started to be replaced by a concept called Kids First Rugby, which says the same things more succinctly).

The Good Players code encourages children to 'play because you want to, not to please coaches or parents' while the Good Spectators code asks adults to 'verbally encourage players in a positive manner, shouting "for" them not "at" them' and recommends adults to 'act as positive role models for children'.

The Good Parents code is almost worth quoting in its entirety, but to save time, here are a few extracts:

- Remember that young people play rugby for their own enjoyment not that of their parents. Encourage young people to play – do not force them.
- Focus on the young players' efforts, rather than winning or losing.

- Be realistic about the young players' abilities; do not push them towards a level that they are not capable of achieving.
- Provide positive verbal feedback both in training and during the game.
- Remember that persistent, negative messages will adversely affect the players' and referee's performance and attitude.
- Always support the rugby club in their efforts to eradicate loud, coarse and abusive behaviour from the game.
- Remember young people learn much by example.
- Always show appreciation of good play by all young players both from your own club and the opposition.
- Respect decisions made by the match officials and encourage the young players to do likewise.

As you can see, all of these are focused on providing an environment that is best for the young players as opposed to the adults on the touchline. Rugby has looked at why children want to play and found that they most enjoy having fun, making friends, learning skills and, of course, post-match hotdogs.

A study by Exeter University analysed children's motivations at far greater length and as a result, from 2008 onwards, the RFU began revising the rules of play for the youngest players to ensure it was a more child-centred game, rather than a cut-down version of adult rugby. Coach education now deals principally with how to enthuse children and ensure they are enjoying the experience, rather than looking specifically at technical aspects of the game.

Coaches therefore are now encouraged to focus less on the result of matches (some coaches find this harder than others, judging by the win/loss ratios some Under 8s teams have on their club website) and more on the performance, how well the players executed their skills and what they can do to get better.

Above all, coaches should try to remember that, in age grade rugby, fun is fundamental, and it's better to have a team that wins some and loses some with smiles on faces than one that always wins but is too intense to enjoy anything other than the result.

Develop with the child

In conclusion, parents and coaches should remember that children view the world differently, and have different value systems and motivations from those that matter to adults. They are playing rugby for their reasons, not yours, and to please themselves, not you. Many parents and even coaches may disagree, but our experience suggests that children only care so much about winning because of the influence of adults.

If you ask children just to play, to enjoy the game and not worry about the score, they perform much better and the score often looks after itself. We've tried this approach, and it works. As players grow and mature, you can adjust the approach to take account of this, and to appeal to their changing needs and motivations, which will become more like those of adults. If coaches can deliver this, supported by parents both on the touchline and in the car or at home, we'll develop future generations of rugby players who love the game for its own sake and play it for pleasure, whether they win or lose.

More than this – if we all regard the score as less important, some of the stress will disappear from the spectators' area, and the bear-pit atmosphere, the referee abuse and the misguided 'touchline coaching' might become a thing of the past. Wouldn't that be something?

5 FOCUS ON PARENTS AND SUPPORTERS

Basics of community rugby

Community rugby is the lifeblood of the sport. It is the grass-roots level of rugby – the place where most players take their first steps into their rugby journey.

Whether a player goes on to represent their club, county, or country could (and in most documented cases is) often forged at those first levels at a community rugby club.

However, the opportunity to represent at a higher level is only a very small part of the picture. Community rugby offers so much more to young players. It is a place where they can take part in active sport – something that is very important in today's society.

Equally, there is a social side to these clubs, an opportunity to interact with other young players from outside the standard social circles of schools or their own local community. This allows for a wider awareness of all sorts of demographics. It allows for friendships to forge that will often outlast those made during school days.

Community rugby covers Under 7s to veterans' rugby, both genders and a variety of versions of the sport. It really is a game for everyone.

Parental support for building the right ethos

Club rugby coaches come in a variety of types. At mini and youth levels you will find a mixture of those who have grown up with the game, played themselves, and now are 'giving something back'; you'll have others who, for whatever reason, moved into coaching earlier;

you may find some current players, encouraged by the club, coaching on a weekend; and you will find other parents of your child's teammates starting their journey into coaching.

One of the key things to remember is that the coaches at a community club will, in the very vast majority, be volunteers. This will be their hobby as much as rugby is hopefully going to be your child's hobby. Rugby coaches have a huge responsibility to embed the core values and standards in their players and, as parents or supporters, you will be there to support that approach. The way in which you encourage your child to take part will be in the games, and training will be the starting point of this journey. These initial steps will have a huge impact on how things play out going forward.

Rugby is a team sport. Individual flair and performance will get some results but working as part of the whole team will always be more successful. So the parental practice, often seen in some other sports, of rewarding a child for scoring, will have a negative impact on the team in the long run. Positive support from the sidelines, not just focusing on your child, will also embed the 'team-spirit' element of what a good coach will be working towards.

Follow the RFU Code of Conduct

As we saw in Chapter 1, the RFU have a five-word view of what rugby is about. They are seen as the CORE VALUES of the sport (see page 10). These five words underpin the codes of conduct that are in place for the game as a whole, and span from the National Team down to every grass-roots club. To remind you, the words are:

- Teamwork
- Respect
- Enjoyment
- Discipline
- Sportsmanship

Collectively referred to as TREDS, these are at the heart of 'the ethos of rugby', or what is referred to as 'the spirit of the game'.

At professional club levels and for national teams, winning is massive; but you will see genuine examples of these core values within that aspect of the sport. Players interacting with opposition after games are obvious moments of respect, mutual appreciation and friendship. These things start at grass-roots level and are embedded in local clubs. They require the support of club coaches, parents, supporters on touchlines and everyone involved in clubs to ensure they remain at the heart of the game.

Why your child wants to play

Children want to play rugby for so many different reasons – whether they have seen a parent play, watched a live game or seen an international match on TV, something has sparked an interest. That is the starting point. They then play for fun, enjoying the sport and the time with their mates on the pitch. In most cases, in the younger age groups this part of the game comes much higher up their list of priorities than winning does. Some research has even found that children actually place the post-match food higher than winning!

As a parent, you may have a different set of reasons. Perhaps your own playing experiences have given you a love of rugby, which you want your offspring to enjoy. You should be mindful that the game has changed in recent years but the ethos you remember will be there. You might have picked the sport for that very reason. The other point is that rugby is a physical sport, lots of running around and activity bound up in things like respect, discipline, teamwork and the like. It has to be better than letting your child just sit around in front of a games console, doesn't it?!

What to expect from your child's coach

Club coaches should first and foremost be qualified and competent. They should have rugby qualifications and, working with their club and the club's coaching co-ordinator, have a personal development plan to enhance their progression as a coach. They will also have passed a DBS check to enable them to work with children. Safeguarding is a big part of all clubs' responsibilities and this is covered in more detail later in this chapter (see page 60–63).

The coach should be organised, have sessions planned, and make rugby engaging, fun, safe and enjoyable for the players. It is their responsibility to show these young players the skills needed for the game while building on the enthusiasm that brought them to the game. They should ensure all players are involved, both in training and in matches. Players do not develop standing on the sidelines and only getting a few minutes' game time.

What is expected of you

As a parent, the key things required of you are to get your child to training and matches on time, communicate with the coach or team manager (another role you could get involved with) and pay the membership fees. Some clubs may have expectations about the match-day kit they expect your child to wear. These will differ from club to club.

Game sense practise session

The main expectation will be for you to get involved. As a spectator, enjoy the matches, praise the players, socialise after the game. The worst thing for a club to see is all of the players, parents and spectators walking off the pitches, getting into their cars and leaving. Rugby is more than just the game and it is those bits of time not playing or training at the club that will pay off later.

Encourage your child to get involved, take part in sessions, listen to their coach, respect their teammates and the opposition on match days. But most of all, enjoy their rugby.

Enthusiasm is a major part. If you don't feel like getting up on the training morning and going to stand out in the rain, wind, sunshine or whatever else the weather decides to do, neither will your child.

How you can help your child's team

As a parent, there are many ways you can help your child's team. These can range from assisting with organising the team on training or match days, writing match reports, recording the names of those attending to far more involvement at their club.

The very basic thing is support. Positive, inclusive, constructive support. Applaud good skills whether it's your child's team or the opposition. This embeds the sportsmanship element of the TREDS (see page 54).

Stepping up a level, you can offer assistance to the coach. This can cover many things:

- You could assist in a coaching role. The club would be grateful for new coaches and the club's coaching co-ordinator would assist you in gaining qualifications (see page 72–73).
- You could help in practical ways such as marking out pitches, collecting cones and filling water bottles.
- Communication is a massive part of running a team and any coach will be grateful for assistance with this. Match reports, well written and positive, encourage and embed the team spirit within the squad. They like seeing their reports in the press or on the club website and this helps to attract other players to the team.
- Administration roles are also part of running a team. The RFU needs players to be registered and keeping up to date with this, together with ensuring that club membership forms and fees are processed, is vital.
- With any sport, there will be a need at some point for a trained first aider, whether for players (your own team or the opposition), supporters, or, in one instance we remember, a referee. If you are trained or have an interest in this aspect, you would be a very welcome addition to the team.
- From a wider point of view, all clubs welcome volunteers and there is a wealth of opportunities in clubs to get involved. Roles such as safeguarding officers, sponsorship managers, social secretaries, fund-raisers, press officers, referees, groundsmen and so many more make up the support infrastructure that allows your child to play rugby on any given day.

Volunteers are the lifeblood of a community rugby club. Without them there are no clubs. This is an opportunity for you to get involved in a community of which you want your child to be part and to help shape their experience of the game.

Parental input and behaviour

Rugby is a team game. While as parents we all focus on our child, this is an environment to try to see past them and look at their involvement in the team.

As a coach, one of the biggest grievances is the habit of parents rewarding their child for scoring a try. Sounds great, a positive reinforcement – but in fact this is the furthest from

Commited tackle

positive we get. What tends to happen is that a child with this reward on their mind is focused solely on scoring as an individual. They get the ball, they run towards the line and, despite support players, will not pass the ball. They end up tackled and stripped of the ball while their teammates look on. Please don't do this as a parent. It is the quickest way to destroy teamwork.

As a parent on the sidelines, be vocal, be positive and acknowledge good play. This involves the opposition too. This is where you have the opportunity to embed those core values mentioned earlier.

Reinforcement

One of the key elements that often has a huge impact on the young player is the time after a training session or game. Coaches have given their teams skills, plans, ideas and maybe structures (as they get older) for playing the game. Our job as a spectator is to do exactly that: watch. However, there is a natural desire to get involved with what our children are doing. It's good to take an interest, to want to be part of what they are doing, as a family. However, this is their game, their time, something for them to embrace and to strive towards.

The first aspect is an ignition. Something that sparks the interest in the sport. It could be having watched dad playing, it might have been a game on the TV. As coaches, the biggest single ignition we witnessed came on the morning of 22 November 2003. A certain Jonny Wilkinson kicked the winning drop goal in the World Cup Final and on the Sunday morning at my club we welcomed 30+ new players. It was that obvious.

The second aspect is harder to pinpoint. It is the desire to get better, the motivation to stick at it, to develop as a player, to put in the hours. A couple of things create that desire in children. Older siblings are handy; they hard-code this desire into the younger child. Watch them play and listen to the words being used. The older child will be telling the younger one to keep up, work harder, try harder and all the normal stuff older brothers and sisters do. But listen to it again from a slightly detached point of view. You see a role model, for that is what the older sibling is, encouraging a younger version to push to excel.

Respect for the opposition and team-mates is at the core of the game

However, all is not lost for the older or single child if they can find an 'I can do that' moment. Again we'll go back to Jonny Wilkinson. Here is a man who the media will tell you won the World Cup. He won't. He never did in the years after that kick and right up to his final match. We dare say he never will.

What you do know about Jonny is that he practised and he put the hours in. The reason: he never ever wanted to let his teammates down and he wanted to get better. In interviews, and there were many, he'd state that he played mini rugby, he trained, he put the hours in and for the right child this is the 'I can do that' ignition moment.

So those are the things that might engage and drive your child to do well in sport. But there remains a risk. And sadly that risk is you, the parent.

The National Alliance for Youth Sports in America has reported that 200,000 children stop playing sport every year. That's *stop* and never start again. The reason for this is exactly the one we discussed on page 47 – that a child's love of the game is eroded if the car ride home involves parental judgement or pressure and negative comments about issues such as coaching tactics, decisions on substitutions, or what another player might have done.

But it's not all bad news. Because there's a second finding to emerge from this, and it might be the best parenting tip we've ever read.

The players reported that there was one phrase spoken by parents that brought them happiness. One simple sentence that made them feel joyful, confident, and fulfilled. Just six words:

'I love to watch you play.'

That's it. Six words that are the exact opposite of the uncomfortable car ride home. Because they reframe your relationship – you stop being the watchful supervisor, and you start being a steady, supportive presence.

'I love to watch you play.'

A signal that sends the simplest, most powerful signal: this is about you. I am your parent, not your coach or your judge. You make me really, really happy.

Try it out. We have. It works.

Safeguarding children

Clubs provide a service to children, families, young adults and others and every one of them deserves to be taking part in rugby in a safe environment. The RFU was at the forefront of carrying out CRB checks – now known as DBS checks (see page 48) – on volunteers who regularly spend time with those individuals.

All clubs are encouraged by the RFU to have in place and publish a safeguarding policy and child protection policy along with a host of other codes of conduct and supporting documents. These items are reviewed and checked by the RFU's Rugby Development Officers and local Community Rugby Coaches.

The bottom line is that clubs take this responsibility seriously and have procedures in place to act on any concerns raised and a complaint heard at a club can be escalated right up to the RFU.

The following is an example of the level of a safeguarding policy, written by co-author Ian for his club:

SAFEGUARDING CHILDREN & VULNERABLE ADULTS POLICY

The Club acknowledges its responsibility to safeguard the welfare of all children and vulnerable adults involved in the Club from harm.

The Club confirms that it adheres to the Rugby Football Union's Safeguarding Policy and the procedures, practices and guidelines and endorses and adopts the Policy Statement contained in that document.

A child is anyone under the age of 18 engaged in any rugby union activity. However, where a 17-year-old male player is playing in the adult game it is essential that every reasonable precaution is taken to ensure his safety and well-being are protected.

The Key Principles of the RFU Safeguarding Children & Vulnerable Adults Policy are as follows:

1. The welfare of the child or vulnerable adult (as appropriate) is, and must always be, paramount to any other considerations.

2. All participants regardless of age, gender, ability or disability, race, faith, culture, size, shape, language or sexual identity have the right to protection from abuse or harm.

3. All allegations or suspicions of abuse, neglect, harm and poor practice will be taken seriously and responded to swiftly, fairly and appropriately.

4. Working in partnership with other organisations, statutory agencies, parents, carers, children and young people is essential for the welfare of children and young people.

5. Children have a right to expect support, and personal and social development delivered by an appropriately recruited, vetted person and managed in relation to their participation in rugby union, whether they are playing, volunteering or officiating in the community or professional areas of the sport.

6. The Club recognises that all children have the right to participate in sport in a safe, positive and enjoyable environment while at the same time being protected from abuse, neglect, harm and poor practice. The Club recognises that this is the responsibility of everyone involved, in whatever capacity, at the club.

7. The Club will implement and comply with the RFU Code of Conduct and the Codes of Conduct for Coaches, Spectators and Officials as appropriate. The Club will ensure its spectators, parents, members and officials are all aware of and have

accepted the club Photographic Policy as set out in the club welcome pack and on the website.

8. The Club will endeavour to comply with the Guidance for Websites as set out on the RFU website and appendixed to this document.

9. The Club Safeguarding Officer is XXXX, whose photograph and contact details appear on the 'Safeguarding' page of the Club's website. If you witness or are aware of an incident where the welfare of a child or vulnerable adult has been put at risk, you must in the first instance inform the Club Safeguarding Officer. They will then inform the CB [Constituent Body] Safeguarding Manager and the RFU Safeguarding Executive. If an incident involves the Club Safeguarding Officer, you should inform the Chairman of the Club's Youth Section and either the CB Safeguarding Manager or the RFU Safeguarding Executive.

10. All members of the Club who have a regular supervisory contact with children or a management responsibility for those working with children must undertake an RFU Enhanced Disclosure and Barring Service disclosure and must also be ISA-registered in accordance with the RFU ISA-registration Policy.

11. The Club will ensure that all its members, whether they are coaches, parents, players or officials, will comply with the Best Practice Guidance as issued by the RFU. In summary, the following are NOT acceptable and will be treated seriously by the club and may result in disciplinary action being taken by the club, the CB or the RFU:

- Working alone with a child, children, vulnerable adult or adults.
- Consuming alcohol while responsible for children or vulnerable adults.
- Providing alcohol to children or allowing its supply.
- Smoking in the presence of children.
- Humiliating children or vulnerable adults.
- Inappropriate or unnecessary physical contact with a child or vulnerable adult.
- Participating in, or allowing, contact or physical games with children or vulnerable adults.
- Having an intimate or sexual relationship with any child or vulnerable adult developed as a result of being in a 'position of trust.'
- Making sexually explicit comments or sharing sexually explicit material.

12. The Club manages the changing facilities and arranges for them to be supervised by two adults (ISA-registered and RFU DBS checked) of the appropriate gender for the players using the facilities. The Club ensures that all its coaches, parents, officials and spectators are aware that adults must not change at the same time, using the same facilities as children or vulnerable adults.

13. The Club will ensure that its coaching staff will receive the support and training considered appropriate to their position and role. The RFU 'Managing Challenging Behaviour' Policy has been adopted and circulated among the club workforce, both voluntary and paid.

14. Any events held on the Club's premises must comply with this Policy and if appropriate a Safeguarding Plan should be discussed and circulated to those affected. Any tours, overseas or domestic, undertaken by the Club must comply with the relevant RFU Regulations and Guidance relating to tours.

6

FOCUS ON COACHES

Different types of coaches/coaching strategies

How we coach is, perhaps, as important as what we coach. We know that people learn in different ways and so one style of coaching may suit one type of learner but not others. So, it is best that a coach varies how they coach according to what and who they are coaching.

There are four main coaching styles and all need to be used according to the situation (remember that how we say things is as important as what we say):

- Tell ('Do as I say.')
- Sell ('If you do what I say it will work.')
- Ask ('How can we solve this problem together?')
- Delegate ('Here is the problem; you need to solve it. I am here if you need me.')

Coaches need to be able to use a range of styles and select the most appropriate for the given participants, context and purpose. No one style is better or worse than any other. There is a time to tell, a time to watch and listen, a time to let participants do more thinking and take more responsibility. Each style will have its place, although some are likely to result in more lasting learning than others. You may demonstrate different styles during a single session.

Research shows that what is said only has a 10 per cent impact on learning, compared with the 90 per cent impact that body language has.

We know from extensive research that players learn most when they are involved in their learning.

When a coach uses a mixture of the 'ask' and 'delegate' styles of coaching, the players learn the most. We call this style of coaching 'player-centred' as opposed to the 'tell' style of coaching, which is more 'coach-centred'.

Holistic Athlete Development issues

As a coach, you have the ability to nurture the development of young people. You'll note that sentence has nothing to do specifically with sport. As a coach, the position you have with the players you are responsible for is unlike most other teaching roles. Players in a team normally all want to be there, they normally all want to develop their skills and they want to play the sport they are there for. You, as coach, are therefore someone they will look to for a wider skill set than just how to pass, tackle and kick.

10 COMMANDMENTS FOR COACHES

1. A great coach is in it for the development of their players, both as rugby players and as people.

2. A great coach never assumes he knows everything, or that he has nothing to learn from the players.

3. A great coach achieves maximum opportunity for player and skills development by finding a balance between coach-centred and player-centred learning that suits the squad as a whole.

4. At the same time, a great coach also recognises that the approach taken at Commandment 3 will not work for certain individuals, and so delivers appropriate development activity to suit these players as well; for example, a more supportive approach with players who are struggling to master a particular skill versus a greater measure of challenge to stretch players who have mastered the skill already.

5. A great coach listens as much as he talks, and asks more questions than he answers – it's preferable for the players to find solutions to their own issues than to have someone else's ideas imposed on them.

6. A great coach does not tolerate prima donna players at whatever age, or allow 'star' players to dominate the team to the detriment of quieter, less pushy players. No one player is more important than any other or than the team as a whole.

7. A great coach will listen to the concerns of players' parents, but will not allow parents to dictate or interfere with on-field matters.

Coach listening to the players and getting the players to lead

8. A great coach will ultimately aim to have his players grow to a level beyond which he can add any value to them – so that they outgrow him naturally as they develop.

9. A great coach will recognise when that moment has come and will hand them over to someone else – even if it is earlier than he had prepared for.

10. Finally, and coaches forget this at their peril, a great coach always remembers that players play rugby because they enjoy playing and so retains an element of fun and enjoyment in training throughout.

How to respond to bad referees

We have a set of modified laws (see page 81–85) for this form of the game, to provide a structured yet simplified framework for the players to display their skills; yet far too many coaches seem to regard a lot of these rules as inconvenient or optional. This can create points of tension and contention whenever your team plays a match against another club and frustrates players when they feel the opposition has been allowed to cheat throughout the game.

There are a number of possible responses to this:

RESPONSE NUMBER 1

Relax your refereeing of the game and allow/encourage your players to infringe in the same way as other teams. This would allow them a level playing field to compete on, but it goes against the grain for us to tell our players it's OK to cheat if it helps them win.

Verdict: We realise that as open-age players they'll be expected to 'play the ref' and to be a bit smart and streetwise about infringing to slow down the opposition. However, we feel that when you're taking players who are new to the game and moulding them into rugby players for the future, you should make every effort to reinforce respect for all facets of the game, including the laws – and for us, that means serial infringers shouldn't be allowed to prosper.

RESPONSE NUMBER 2

Just chill out and ignore it. Different referees interpret the laws differently; our players have to learn to accept this, and as coaches we have to set the example for them to follow. Any frustration we feel needs to be hidden and we ought to focus on what our players can do to outflank the opposition, even if the referee is letting them infringe.

Verdict: We would agree with all of that – except for the fact that our players deserve better, and when they know that the referee is getting it wrong, their coach is the one they ask why. Somehow, 'never mind the ref, look at your own performance' seems a little too harsh a message to give to a seven-year-old. In any case, it's not as if the laws for Under 8s rugby are especially complicated or difficult to referee correctly, so surely it's not too much to ask that a referee be more than just vaguely competent?

RESPONSE NUMBER 3

Approach the referee in question, say at half-time, and request clarification on why infringements are or are not being dealt with. For example, ask: 'I notice you're not pinging them for handing-off, sir – does that mean our players can do it too?'

Verdict: This is fraught with difficulty. Some referees will take your oblique point and will clamp down on the relevant offence for the rest of the game, and will be happy that you've brought it to their attention. This is a definite win. However, other referees will take your intervention as a personal criticism and a rather tetchy exchange then ensues from which no one will emerge the winner.

We had one of these at a well-known festival in the south of England, in which a neutral referee was great at pinging our Under 7s players for not passing within three steps after being tagged, but terrible at penalising the opposition for shoulder-barging players out of the way.

At half-time it was politely requested that he stop them from doing it; he replied very shortly that he was the referee and we did not have the right to tell him how to referee the game and he hadn't seen the offence in question. Not a successful outcome, then, and one that probably left each of us looking at the other and thinking 'Self-righteous numpty!'

RESPONSE NUMBER 4

Never to allow anyone but yourself referee your games – just not practical, and in some cases not necessary as a number of referees are every bit as good as you, or nearly so!

Verdict: No, the only solution that is really acceptable is to get all coaches at your age group to referee using all the modified laws, rather than ignoring certain ones to give their team an advantage. It's the only way to ensure a level playing field for both teams in a match.

'Local variations' can mean that in some cases your team is asked to play a vastly different set of rules than they are used to. A few years ago, our 'tag' age groups toured the north-east and on starting their first match at their festival on the Sunday were surprised to find a 'double-tag' rule in operation, whereby ripping off both an opponent's tags at once gave you an immediate turnover.

All the Northumbrian teams were aware of the rule, but it took our players some time to adapt. Not all differences are as pronounced, but it is true to say that every time we play a match, the laws used are slightly different from the previous game.

For youngsters learning the game and the skills to play it, this kind of inconsistency needs to be stamped out. We've met coaches who justify a lax approach to refereeing minis' rugby on the grounds that 'They're only kids' (i.e. they shouldn't be burdened with being expected to follow the rules of the game).

So why do you think the laws are there? The fact is, the simplified laws for tag rugby are designed for children to be able to follow. Yes, it might be difficult and onerous to get it across, but with time and persistence, it's definitely achievable. And once the habit is formed, it gets easier to help the players adapt to the laws as they change with the different stages along the age grade pathway.

It might be that constituent bodies (the local sub-groups of the RFU) and Rugby Development Officers need to give some thought to minis' rugby refereeing as part of a coach's skill set so that we get more competent referees working with the youngest players, then match day will stop being a lottery based on what rules the home side thinks should apply.

WHY I BECAME A RUGBY COACH

For this section, it might be easier to explain why I became a coach. This is therefore my story. I'm Ian Milligan and this is how I became involved in rugby. I took my eldest son to rugby when he was five years old after watching an England match with him. This was his ignition moment. The opportunity to try mini rugby was given to him the next day following a chance encounter with a gentleman who changed our lives as a family and introduced us to community rugby. Richard Palmer was the youth chairman at what is now my club.

So I took my son to that club and stood and watched for a week or so before one of the coaches asked if I'd help out. So DBS forms done and a rugby coaching course booked, I started my journey as a coach.

The reason in my head was this was something we – dad and son – could do together. And so the biggest challenge as a coach started. Parents as coaches fall into two camps:

1. Focused firstly on their child. These coaches pick their offspring in the position they believe they should play and build the team around them.

2. Focused as a coach on the team. All players developed and their offspring treated the same as every other player.

I worked hard to be in the second camp – to the point where, at rugby, my son doesn't call me 'Dad'. We stop that at the car park and pick it up as we leave the club on the way home. He got substituted the same as every other player, played in a number of positions and was treated the same as every other player on the pitch. Or at least I tried to ensure this was the case. I'm sure that there was more I could have done but that is the second point of coaching.

After a season or two, this became not just somewhere to spend time with my son but my hobby too. And I wanted to be the best I could be. I signed up for courses and researched approaches to coaching and worked to be the best I could be. I'm still working on that.

Aims of coaching age grade rugby

In mini rugby there are those who believe that winning is the be all and end all of everything. The seven-year-old players are drilled to do this and that in a 'play rugby by numbers' approach and really have no idea of what they are doing. Coaches yell instruction on to the pitch and dissect the game afterwards. These clubs might have loads of players at mini rugby level and they might win a lot of games, but there is a risk here. Remember the reinforcement section earlier. Clubs like this see a huge drop-off in numbers around 12 years old and this continues through the youth age groups, so that when the children reach 17 or 18 there is only a handful moving up into the senior part of the club.

Simply put, the single aim in coaching age grade rugby is to help the players be better this week than they were last and to have a plan to do that again next week. It isn't about winning at Under 8s. Remember the players are there to have fun, spend time with their friends, and they actually care more about the food after the game than the result! Now, that doesn't mean they want to lose, so this is where the coach comes in: if you develop the players to have the skills and the ability to use them without having to shout from the sidelines, the results will look after themselves.

Continuous development

In England, the following are the requirements for coaching rugby:

DBS CHECK
The Disclosure and Barring Service (DBS) check is done every three years to ensure the individual is fit to work with children or vulnerable adults. This is normally undertaken by the club's Safeguarding Officer and is now processed online. The RFU covers the cost for this check and the outcome is recorded on the Rugby First system, to which clubs have access. The RFU will not accept a DBS check from another sport or profession.

RUGBY READY COURSE
The next step for coaching, once the DBS check is signed off, is the Rugby Ready course. This is not really a coaching course, although it has basic aspects of coaching within it; instead, it aims to educate, aid and support players, coaches, match officials and Unions on the importance of sufficient preparation to avoid any injury during training and matches.

SCRUM FACTORY CPD
Next in line is now the Scrum Factory CPD (Continuous Personal Development) course.

This course aims to develop safe and effective eight-player scrummaging as an integral part of the game at all levels. It works up from the single player body position, showing good practice; introduces the latest developments in scrum coaching; and builds towards increasing confidence in coaching the eight-player scrum.

The more formal qualifications are now split into the Level 1 and Level 2 courses as starting points:

UKCC LEVEL 1: COACHING CHILDREN RUGBY UNION

The Level 1 course is now referred to as UKCC Level 1: Coaching Children Rugby Union. It is an entry level course for coaches of children and offers guidance on developing the whole child through the game. It will qualify you to coach and referee (game coaching) children in Rugby Union; through your work you will be better able to develop core skills and core values in young players in an active, purposeful, enjoyable and safe environment.

UKCC LEVEL 2: COACHING THE XV-A-SIDE GAME

The Level 2 course or UKCC Level 2: Coaching the XV-a-Side Game is intended to advance those coaches who may have been working with children in rugby union and now begin the transition into the 15-a-side game. It also acts as an entry to the qualification programme for those coaches who are currently coaching 15-a-side rugby, but have not been involved in coaching children rugby union.

This course aims to give coaches the skills to:

- Deliver rugby union coaching sessions and provide direction to other coaches.
- Understand the principles of coaching.
- Know how to plan, establish and maintain a safe coaching environment.
- Understand how to plan and support the delivery of activities that are age and stage appropriate for players.
- Understand how to evaluate coaching activities and how to evaluate your own coaching practice.

Running alongside the qualification courses are a series of CPD courses for coaches. These range from the basic skills to the much more complex courses and are designed to meet the needs of coaches at different stages of their development. The club's co-ordinator will have access to the details of courses and will work with the coach to develop their own plan.

The RFU are looking to bring coach licensing into force for clubs and this will require coaches to undertake a recognised CPD course within a set time frame to ensure their knowledge remains up to date.

Outside all of these rugby courses there is much to be learned from researching other sports, watching other coaches delivering sessions and working with mentors. A good coach will want to continue to develop themselves.

Coaching boys vs coaching girls

Boys and girls train and play together in mini rugby; however, training these two groups demands different skills from a coach. Often, if you give a group of boys a task, they will run off and execute what they think they just heard. Give the same task to a group of girls and they normally ask you a number of questions about it, including the desired outcome, reason behind the drill, etc. They go away and execute it and then wonder why you want them to repeat it if they have done it right the first time. Girls can also respond to certain types of communication better than boys, including more positive reinforcements.

Coaches should not demonstrate with players. Use an assistant coach if needed

Obviously, these are very general comments and different children react differently, but it helps to underline that as a coach you need to adapt your method, communication and approach for the specific group of players you are working with.

This point carries on into more senior levels of men's and women's rugby coaching as girls mature faster than boys and may respond to different styles of coaching better than others.

Transition points

The pathway for players from mini to adult is set up in stages. Under 7s and Under 8s play tag rugby (see page 85) before having a few contact skills introduced on a stepped basis as they progress into Under 9s and upwards. The New Rules of Play (NRoP) have been rolled out to stagger these aspects of the game to allow children and coaches to focus and develop individual skills before moving on to the next step.

This does mean that it takes a while for the game to become what they see on the TV, but it allows for skills-based coaching to focus on the numerous elements of the game in a gradual progression.

The transition points have a number of law variations, which are covered in the rules section of the book (see page 79), but at a high level these points are split as follows:

- Under 7s and Under 8s rugby – played as non-contact tag rugby.

- Under 9s to Under 12s – introduction to contact. Starting at Under 9s, the tackle is introduced into the game, and gradually after that the ruck, maul, line-out and scrum are introduced as the size of the pitch increases to half a full pitch. The number of players increases in each year range and finishes at Under 12s where the teams are 13 a side.

- Under 13s to Under 15s – played on a full-sized pitch with 15 players per side. Scrum halves have to stay at the tunnel of the scrum for a non-attacking team; there is no lifting in the line-out.

- Under 16s to Under 18s is played with all laws as in the adult game, with the exception of the 'squeeze ball', when the ball carrier places the ball between his legs after a tackle; lifting is allowed in line-outs.

Elite player development

While we have focused on the community game in the majority of this section, there still exists the part of the game to develop elite players.

From around 12 years old, opportunities exist for players to develop at a higher level than club rugby. Most constituent bodies, which are the areas the clubs are in, have representative teams. These teams select players from across the clubs in the area to represent them in inter-area games.

As further opportunities for young players, there are often Elite Player Development Centres, run in conjunction with Premiership rugby teams, where talented players are invited to further their rugby development. As rugby is a late-development sport, these opportunities are reviewed annually.

There is a pathway in place for player development; this involves, but is not restricted to: club rugby, representative rugby (county), representative rugby (constituent body), professional club training group, national age groups. Alongside this pathway is also one that runs via educational bodies, college rugby, England colleges, etc.

The other route to progression is being 'spotted', and the following is a fine example of this. A young player attending a Leicester Tigers summer rugby club was 'spotted' by their lead coach at 14 years old. The coach saw something in this young man; asked what it was, the coach defined it as 'coachability'.

The young player transferred his education to the Tigers Academy. He developed, and at age 17 he was signed for Tigers as a prop forward. His first starting shirt hangs in the clubhouse of the club where he began his rugby career.

Communicating with parents and supporters

Communication within a rugby club is a challenge. There are many sections of the club and a lot of things to communicate to a lot of different people.

Most clubs have their own websites and this is a great way to get details of events, matches, training and many other things out to members. If your team does not already have a website, they can obtain a free website through Pitchero (www.pitchero.com) and teams can also advertise to new players and potential opposition for free on FindRugbyNow's website (www.findrugbynow.com).

With the rise of social media, most clubs will also have a presence on Facebook and Twitter and will use these media tools to advertise upcoming events at the club.

Every rugby club will be different, but normally coaches can utilise different media outlets like Chairman's reports, club newsletters, committee meetings, annual general meetings and weekly team emails to get their news across to parents and coaches. Some coaches and team managers prefer to communicate directly with parents via email or text messages.

Aside from the more usual forms of communication by email or phone, there are some great rugby apps to assist coaches with managing team availabilities, such as Teamer (http://teamer. net/), an event notification system that uses email, text messages and mobile app notifications to allow you to liaise with parents/players about upcoming training sessions and matches. Team App (http://teamapp.com/) can help you create a mobile app customised to your team, which will allow you to share information with parents and players.

Just check that your preferred mode of communication matches your club's/team's policies and suitability standards.

Planning a session

It is good practice for coaches to plan their sessions in advance. This has two main benefits. Firstly, it provides notes that can be reviewed during the session as a memory jogger, and secondly, it provides a resource for later use and to review the session just delivered.

A coaching plan can consist of a few simple notes or something much more involved, with diagrams, equipment notes and much more. The trick is to make it work for you. Having the odd note to refer to during a session is useful but pulling pages of detailed diagrams out on a muddy pitch is not a workable solution. It also has the potential to make it look like you don't know what you are doing.

There are a number of resources available to a coach who is looking to plan sessions. Online libraries of drills, exercises and examples of best practice are available with a little help from a good search engine; some examples are provided in the following section.

A sample training template is available on the IRB website: http://www.irbcoaching.com/downloads/L1_session_planning_templates_EN.pdf

Coaching tools

There is a variety of great tools now available to coaches to assist with planning rugby sessions and recording team results and development.

One of our favourite mobile phone apps is the Rugby Reporter (http://rugby.matchreporter. net/), which allows coaches to keep track of key elements of the rugby match including the time, score and team progress and then supplement this with a written report that they can post directly to Facebook or publish via email.

Another great tool available is G.A.P.S. Rugby Union Coaching Software which helps coaches to plan training sessions. The software includes over 250 animated games and drills, with detailed explanations covering: passing and handling, defence, rucking, mauling, line-out, scrimmage, kicking, FUNdamental games and many others. What we like about the software is that it allows you as a coach to plan your session right then and there by picking and choosing drills and allowing you to take notes, which you can then print and take with you to the session.

The session planner also prompts coaches to choose aims and desired outcomes for the session, which automatically encourages them to think more deeply about the drills they are selecting. Coaches can even save planned sessions, enabling them to plan ahead for weeks at a time if they wish, and they can add notes to a drill or session after it is completed, for future use.

An interesting addition to the software is a Risk Assessment component which can be of great use to both coaches and clubs by reinforcing the safety aspect of sessions, often not considered enough at a grass-roots level.

There are many other great rugby apps to assist coaches, so please do check out your mobile App Store.

7

THE LAWS OF RUGBY

Fundamentals

At whatever level or format being played, the game of rugby will include the following basic principles.

AIM

The aim of the game is to score tries, worth 5 points, by placing the ball on the ground on or behind the opponent's goal-line. In many forms of the game, additional points can be scored by kicking at the posts, but the principal aim remains to score tries.

METHOD OF PLAY

The team in possession carries the ball in hand. Ball carriers can run forward, evading opponents, who can attempt to stop them by tackling or touch/tag-tackling. Only the player holding the ball may be tackled.

In rugby union, it is a fundamental principle that in all phases of the game, including at the tackle, the opposition is allowed to contest for the ball (i.e. try to pick it up).

Players may pass the ball by hand to a teammate, but the ball must travel sideways or backwards (towards the goal-line of the team in possession) from where it was passed. If the ball is thrown or dropped in a forward direction (a 'knock-on'), possession passes to the opponent.

The ball may also be kicked from hand in many variants of the game; the kick may travel in any direction the kicker chooses (usually forward).

Players must stay on their team's side of the ball, otherwise they are offside and may not take part in the game. For the team in possession, this means all supporting players must be level with or behind the line of the ball/ball carrier. A player who is in front of the kicker when a ball is kicked forward is also offside.

FIELD OF PLAY

The field of play is rectangular and enclosed by the touchlines (along the long sides of the field) and the goal-lines (across the shorter ends).

Play must take place within the field of play. If a player carries, kicks or throws the ball out of play over the touchline (ball in touch), possession passes to the opposition.

SUBSTITUTION

The laws also stipulate the number of players allowed per team and how substitution of players should be made. In the youngest age groups, players can be substituted as desired by coaches (rolling substitution) as long as this happens during a break in play and the referee is informed. In older age groups, rolling substitution may apply for club friendly games, but for teams playing in League or Cup competitions, players usually have to stay off the field once substituted. The only time they would be allowed back on is in the event of subsequent injuries to other players, leaving the team short of specialist players like props. To ensure that scrums remain safe, a previously replaced prop would be allowed back on to the field so the scrum could be played with suitably trained players.

There are many more laws that govern conduct of the game, but these are the basic ones common to all the forms of rugby described in this book.

Development tool

If you look at elite rugby in the 1980s and compare it to the game played today, one of the things you'll notice is that the game's laws have undergone radical change in the intervening years. In part, these changes have been driven by player safety – the scrum engagement sequence in its various guises since 2009 is a good example – but since the advent of professionalism, World Rugby has been equally concerned with selling the game to sponsors and TV networks. As a result, many law changes are designed to speed up the game and make it more of a spectacle that appeals to the viewer at home, as well as TV executives.

The game is also now more safety-conscious than of old, a matter of necessity due to players being far bigger, faster and more powerful than they were back then.

It has been argued that the law of unintended consequences has operated consistently in recent years, meaning that World Rugby law amendments have achieved the opposite effect to that desired. The constant need to bring in more revenue via TV and sponsorship deals means that the governing bodies are constantly looking for ways to tinker with the game and make it the ultimate spectator sport to attract new audiences. However, they need to balance this against the needs of the players. They need to be careful that the game does not evolve too far and too fast as there is a hard core of traditional rugby supporters, many of them ex-players, who love the game just fine the way it is (or the way it used to be, in many cases!). These are the people who go to club games week in and week out and who thereby help to support the grass-roots game that forms the foundations of the rugby pyramid (with community club at the base and the elite game at the top).

What applies to the pinnacle of the game also holds true in the case of the laws as they apply to age grade rugby, in that they have a crucial role in ensuring that players can enjoy the game in safety while providing an exciting spectacle for the parents on the touchline.

However, the modified laws for age grade rugby also provide coaches with a vital tool for educating their young players in the niceties of the game. It therefore behoves coaches to be thoroughly versed in the laws as they apply to the age group they are coaching, and also to be proficient in applying the laws in a coaching scenario.

In the remainder of this chapter, we'll explore the current age grade law variations applying in England[20] to illustrate how these assist in framing the player development pathway, and also discuss two other key aspects: how to incorporate the laws into coaching activity, and how to referee age grade rugby using the laws to assist players' understanding of the game.

While much of this content is intended for coaches, it should also help parents of young players to achieve a greater understanding of the various law variations and why they are so important to players' development.

Laws for age grade rugby

The development of a distinct set of laws for children's rugby has obvious advantages that few would deny. Certainly, no one advocates very young players being asked to play 15-a-side on a full-size pitch for 80 minutes.

As children are smaller than adults, and less physically developed, they are less well able to cope with the demands of the 'uncut' version of the game. It stands to reason, therefore, that children need their own version. From around 1990 and up until 2008, the RFU in England addressed this need via the playing regulations of the Continuum. These provided children with a gradual introduction to rugby as played by adults, starting with tag rugby to encourage running, handling and evasion skills, and gradually building on the contact elements of the game from Under 9s upwards. In essence, what they produced from Under 11s and above was a miniaturised version of the adult game, with most of the elements in place from Under 9s onwards (see summary in Table 7.1).

As a coach, this provided a good structure for building skills progressively over the years as each new element of the game was introduced, though the sudden leap to 'complete' rugby at Under 9s was a challenge, to say the least. However, one great disadvantage was that from a very early age, young players were introduced to a game full of specialist technical requirements (scrums and line-outs), where there was often more emphasis on winning the contest at the breakdown than on what to do with the ball once it re-emerged from a ruck or maul (see pages 168–170).

As only the biggest, strongest or most physically assertive players enjoyed these more robust parts of the game, you could often find players reduced to the status of bystanders while their teammates wrestled over possession. Occasionally you might get the formation of a huge, near-static maul involving almost every player on the pitch, lurching this way and that until the referee blew up for a scrum, from which another maul would soon form, and so on.

However, what children enjoy most about rugby is open play; space to run into, opponents to tackle, teammates in support to pass to, and above all, scoring tries.

One issue with these variations of the game was that they had largely the same laws in play as the adult version. For example, just as in an international game, it was possible for an Under 9s player to be penalised for any one of 19 infringements at the ruck, and impossible as a coach to ensure your players were au fait with all the laws for this and every other phase of the game.

When age grade rugby was refereed under the Continuum, to help the players learn and develop referees often had to strike a balance between allowing the game to flow, being sympathetic to the stage of development the players were at, and ensuring it didn't descend into a free-for-all where almost nothing was penalised. In terms of providing an enjoyable game for the children, the Continuum regulations simply contained too many laws for the level of skill on display. This meant infringements were frequent, and many had to be ignored for the game to progress – the flip side of this being that one set of parents or the other would feel the referee was letting the opposition get away with murder.

Consistency in applying the laws was one way to mitigate this, but differences in emphasis by individual coaches on this area of the laws meant that when one club played another it

TABLE 7.1 Key differences in rules between age groups on the RFU Continuum, c. 1990–2008

Age	Teams	Pitch (m)	Ball	Tackling	Ruck/Maul	Scrum	Lineout	Kicking
U7	7-a-side (plus on-field coach)	50 x 30	Size 3	Tag[1]	None	None	None	None
U8[2]		55 x 30						
U9	9-a-side	60 x 35				3 v 3 uncontested	2 v 2 uncontested	
U10		60 x 35				3 v 3[3]	2 v 2	
U11	12-a-side	65 x 40	Size 4	Tackle	Yes; no limits on players involved	5 v 5	4 v 4	Open play, conversions
U12	13-a-side	65 x 45				6 v 6	5 v 5	
U13[4]								
U14	15-a-side	Up to full size				8 v 8 limited contest	7 v 7 limited contest[5]	Unrestricted
U15			Size 5					
U16								

NOTES

[1] Tag belts should conform to standards specified in Regulations, both teams using belts or tags of equal specification.

[2] To reward good defence, a six-tag rule MAY be used in agreement between coaches.

[3] Contested scrums start at U10; however, until U19 age group there are limitations on the distance a scrum can be pushed (1.5m maximum) and on how far it can wheel (no more than 45°).

[4] At U13, players are allowed to fend/hand off opponents; at U12 and below this should not be permitted.

[5] Lifting in the lineout not permitted below U16.

could seem to the away team like a completely alien set of laws. Needless to say, this caused some contention and criticism.

A common complaint was for (correctly) penalising players below Under 13s for handing off. This source of conflict exemplified the problem with the 'too many rules' form of the game. There were so many technical infringements to watch for that many coaches felt that to blow up for a hand-off was unnecessarily spoiling the players' fun. However, the reason for the rule being there for the youngest age groups was to ensure the safety and enjoyment of all players, vital for those children taking their first steps in the game. Imagine a nervous eight-year-old playing his first ever full-contact match; he keeps trying to tackle his opponents but each time he gets swatted away with a hand in the face. Quite apart from the risk of fingers in eyes, this kind of discouraging experience is not going to build confidence or develop a love of the game – on the contrary, a few weeks of this is enough to drive a child out of rugby completely. The solution is to stop players handing off, which shouldn't prevent them enjoying the game whatsoever – while at the same time giving smaller, less assertive players the chance to develop technique in safety.

In essence, the old format of the age grade game, while preferable to having children playing full-pitch rugby, was nonetheless basically a reduced version of adult rugby. Nowhere was this clearer than in the preponderance of laws dealing with technique, which led to a tendency for referees to ignore some of the laws designed to ensure safety, for fear of being seen as 'whistle-happy'. Having so many laws also meant that the players had so many more opportunities to infringe and 'get it wrong' – another critical demotivating factor and one that only the most empathetic coaches were able to surmount.

NEW RULES OF PLAY

In the mid-2000s, concerned at the high drop-out rate of players between the ages of 16 and 23, the RFU commissioned a study into youth players' motivations for playing, in the hope of instilling greater enjoyment and a lasting love of the game. This led to the adoption in 2008 of a pilot scheme known as Shaping The Game, run initially in three counties across England, and gradually rolled out to the rest over the following five years as the New Rules of Play.

These are now in use at Under 10s downwards across the whole of England, and in many areas they encompass Under 11s and Under 12s as well.

As Table 7.2 shows, the introduction of technical skills now happens later and more gradually; at the youngest age groups, teams are significantly smaller, giving each child more chance to be involved in play. From Under 9s upwards, the pitch size is much the same as previously, meaning that with fewer players on the field, there's far more space for everyone to play. Other innovations to encourage children to play include removing the forward pass and knock-on rules at Under 7s – fewer infringements, therefore fewer stoppages, not to mention taking away the feeling of failure for players who drop the ball and lose possession for their team. Now it's just a call of 'play on' and the first team to react to the game situation gets the ball. Having initially been sceptical about these new rules, once we saw them in action at a coaches' workshop they immediately made sense; the Under 7s played a fast-flowing end-to-end game of rugby with lots of tries being scored and the referee's whistle rarely used. Every player was involved throughout and, at the end, all had clearly enjoyed the game hugely. It was a striking demonstration of how applying a simple and sensible variation of the laws could create a version of the game that children would love, and that allows them plenty of scope to try out and develop both technical and tactical skills.

TABLE 7.2   Key differences in rules between age groups under the RFU New Rules of Play, 2008–present

Age	Teams	Pitch (m)	Ball	Tackling	Ruck/Maul	Scrum	Lineout	Kicking
U7[1]	4-a-side[2]	20 x 12	Size 3	Tag[3]	None	None	None	None
U8[2]	6-a-side[2]	40 x 25						
U9	7-a-side	60 x 30		Tackle[4]				
U10	8-a-side	60 x 30	Size 4	Tackle	1 v 1 mini-ruck/maul	3 v 3 uncontested		No goal kicks
U11	9-a-side	60 x 35			2 v 2 mini-ruck/maul			
U12	10-a-side	60 x 40				5 v 5 uncontested		
U13[5]	15-a-side	Up to full size			No restriction[6]	8 v 8 limited contest[7]	7 v 7 limited contest[8]	No restriction
U14								
U15			Size 5					
U16								

NOTES

[1] Forward passes and knock-ons are not penalised, allowing play to flow.

[2] At U7 and U8, the on-field coach for each team is replaced by one referee/coach who assists both teams. Smaller teams mean each player is more involved in the game.

[3] Tag belts should conform to standards specified in Regulations, both teams using belts and tags of equal specification.

[4] In addition to approved techniques, a 'grab tackle' is introduced at U9 to allow less confident tacklers to contribute in defence. To reward good defence, a six-tackle rule MAY be used by agreement between coaches.

[5] As with the Continuum, handing/fending off is allowed only from U13 upwards.

[6] The reduced ruck and maul up to U12 allows coaches to focus on building correct technique in this vital area of the game, and encourages players to get the ball away faster rather than focus on the contest itself.

[7] The use of small uncontested scrums up to U13 allows coaches to focus on building correct technique rather than on winning the contest through power and aggression. This is a major benefit for player safety.

[8] The later introduction of the lineout removes another technical, specialised area from the game and allows players to focus on wider skills development for longer.

Application of the laws

Having looked at how law changes can influence the structure of the game, it's also worth noting that how coaches and referees apply the laws in training and match situations can make a huge difference to a young player's approach to the game. This is especially true of the positive effect that judicious use of the laws can have on an individual player's attitude, and also on that of teams as a whole – if we think back to the chapter on the ethos of the game, it's fair to say that your desired ethos will dictate how you apply the laws, and this in turn will further refine the ethos of the team.

Our careers as referees and coaches have provided us with ample opportunity to test this theory, and experience would tend to back us up. Here are a couple of illustrations of how the laws can be used as a positive player-development tool.

When coaching players in the tackle phase of the game, especially on actions after the tackle (when a ruck forms), keeping the laws in mind can help in ensuring players use the correct technique. This is not simply about stopping them from joining from the side, though that should be encouraged.

More specifically, when looking at a player's body angle driving through the ruck, the best technique for delivering the power of the drive into contact (straight back, flexed knees, head straight and eyes looking forward) matches the body position stipulated in the laws.[21] So when you're coaching the correct body posture, not only can you tell players that this is the best method for driving powerfully over the ball, you can also underline that if they do straighten their legs and bend their back, not only will their drive be weak but they also stand a chance of being penalised.

The same principle can be applied to many other phases of the game, such as the put-in to the scrum, catching a high ball and pretty much anything that happens in the line-out. It's one thing telling players their technique was wrong and that doing it the correct way next time will be more likely to lead to a successful outcome. Emphasising this point by reference to consequences under the laws reinforces the learning point and gives the player a greater incentive to do it right in future – and has the added benefit of helping players to learn the laws as they go along.[22]

In their additional role of referee, coaches can also use the laws to improve players' understanding and skills base. This being so, coaches should look upon the task of refereeing as a core coaching skill, rather than an onerous burden. In training sessions, different approaches to refereeing can be adopted to achieve different ends. For example, if you're trying to get your players out of a particular bad habit, such as running back towards their own try-line in an effort to find space, there is no better way to do this than simply 'pinging' them out of it.

This was an issue one of us had with an Under 9s squad a few years ago, so after a few weeks we introduced a law variation in training games whereby running backwards became a penalty. It didn't take too many turnovers per side for the players to realise that the best way to keep the ball was to go forward and look for support. Similarly, the following season the same squad was losing a lot of its own ruck ball, until we identified that the players arriving in support were trying to pick the ball up instead of driving the defenders back. So in training, we were really strict on hands in the ruck, and designated one player on each team to make the clearing pass. Any infringements were penalised, and on each occasion we took the opportunity to explain to players how to avoid getting pinged next time. In time, the players focused on clearing away opponents so the scrum half could come in and play the ball, and the turnover issue went away.

Refereeing

Matches are another case entirely; when refereeing your team against another club, it's in no way appropriate to start fiddling around with the laws, as the opposition won't have a clue what's going on. This does happen by accident, however, as most coaches when refereeing have certain laws that they don't like to enforce, as with the example of the hand-off discussed above. Most coaches and players will accept a referee being generally a bit slack all round, or consistently overlooking offences by both teams whether through having missed them or through the application of 'materiality' (this is when, in the referee's opinion, an infringement doesn't 'materially affect play', so he can simply ignore it as having no bearing on the game; it is NOT the same as advantage, see page 88). However, no one likes to feel that the referee is using a set of rules that they or their players aren't familiar with. The people who like this least are the most important people in the game – the players on the pitch.

As the referee's job is to ensure first the safety and then the enjoyment of all players, it stands to reason that the game should be officiated equitably above all. The only way to ensure this is to referee the game as closely as possible to the published laws. If this is done in training games as well as club matches, the players will get used to playing to the laws under match conditions. Whenever you blow your whistle to stop the game, you should always explain your decision to the players and preferably loudly enough (with appropriate hand signals) for the spectators to know what's going on.

This explanation is crucial, so the players understand what was done wrong and more importantly how to do it right next time. In this way, the referee acts as a coach to both teams, reinforcing the skills they learn in training and promoting their understanding of the laws, and of how referees apply them – crucial to their effectiveness for players as they get older.[23]

Finally, we should mention the most important law of all when refereeing age grade rugby;

the law of advantage, which is used when an offence has occurred that should be penalised but when to do so would deny the non-offending side the chance to profit. Proper use of the advantage law keeps the game flowing, while at the same time ensuring that those infringements that need to be 'pinged' are kept in mind and dealt with as required.

This adds to the enjoyment of players in three main ways: a game that keeps flowing is more fun than one that stops and starts all the time; a game where infringing (or 'cheating', as many youngsters like to call it) is dealt with appeals to the players' sense of what's fair; and lastly, it underlines the laws without which the game would be chaos, reinforcing the boundaries that players value so much.

The only time the advantage law would not be applied is in the case of serious foul play, when the game may need to be stopped straight away to attend to an injury – and, of course, to deal with the offender in the appropriate way.

Refereeing is a huge pleasure if you're doing it well, not because you're always involved in the game but because you need to intervene relatively rarely and the game flows. The guidelines laid out in this chapter are a good place to start; admittedly they aim at a high standard of refereeing, but players deserve no less than the best. We know from experience as parents and coaches how frustrating players find it when the referee either seems biased or doesn't know what he's doing. So learn the laws and the relevant variations, apply them with consistency, common sense, communication and liberal use of advantage, don't overlook dissent (it does the player no favours in the long run) and, above all, keep your sense of humour. With a bit of luck, by following this code you'll enjoy refereeing age grade rugby as much as we do.[24]

REFEREE SIGNALS

World Rugby has devised a range of hand signals that referees use to communicate their decisions to players and spectators. These reinforce verbal explanations (and add a little theatre to the game, enhancing it as a spectacle in our humble opinion).

We like to use these even when refereeing age grade games because, by doing so, we get the players used to seeing them and understanding what they mean. Even if they can't hear us shouting in the hurly-burly of a match, the hand signal should tell them what is afoot.

The most important signals for a player or spectator to recognise are:

- Penalty – arm raised towards the side awarded the penalty.

- Try – arm raised in the air with a blast on the whistle.

- Knock-on – hand moved back and forward to simulate patting a ball in the direction indicated.

- Advantage – arm straight out to the side, towards the team to whom advantage has been awarded.

BECOME A REFEREE

Most referees in age grade rugby have traditionally been the coach of the home team, an experienced ex-player with the requisite grasp of the laws and the respect of the players. If our clubs are anything to go by, there is a move to get more and more of these willing amateurs properly qualified as referees, to enhance their skills in managing the game and providing a great experience for the players.

Dave Beal followed this path himself via two separate RFU refereeing courses, so wholeheartedly endorses this theory.

'Doing the course will make you a better referee, because it teaches you the importance of game management and, through this, makes you more confident when you step on the pitch. You feel like you're in charge; this represents a nice contrast to my first experience of refereeing age grade rugby, a chaotic Under 7s fixture that I almost lost control of because the players picked up on my nervousness and felt uneasy themselves. What made this go away was plenty of experience through practice, backed by a solid qualification in how to run a game.

If you want to come over to the dark side and join the ranks of age grade referees, the best place to start is to get some experience refereeing games of touch or tag rugby. Small-sided games are best as, with fewer players, you can see more readily what goes on. If you referee games in training sessions you lose the pressure of the scoreboard and can make decisions in the secure knowledge you won't get barracked from the touchline. The most important skill to learn is to manage the game; all elite referees do this and if you watch the RBS 6 Nations on television, you'll hear the instructions they give players. The idea is to be proactive in telling the players what to do, so that they don't get to the point of committing an infringement, and the game can be allowed to flow uninterrupted by whistling. At every phase of the game and especially the breakdown (ruck or maul) I know what I want the players to do, I ask them to do it, and if they don't comply then I play advantage and if none accrues, then the whistle blows and we come back to the infringement. With clear and timely communication and the cooperation of the players, effective game management makes the difference between a good game and a bad one.'

Once you feel confident with the process of managing the game, think about going on a course. The RFU runs the Entry Level Refereeing Award (ELRA), which is open to candidates aged 14 and upward. A combination of multimedia instruction, workbook exercises, discussion and practical work outside (bring boots and a gumshield!) left me feeling full of confidence in my ability to referee adult as well as junior games. Starting at ELRA levels 1 & 2 (I took a combined course), on completion you are a bona fide rugby referee and the proud possessor of red and yellow cards and an Acme™ 'Thunderer' whistle. The key here is to gain more experience as soon as you can. Referee some junior rugby to start with and if you feel comfortable there, you can take on an adult game or two.

The next step up the ladder is Level 3, at which point you become a fully fledged Society referee (i.e. a member of your local Referees' Society). To make this transition, you need to complete five matches, filling in a self-evaluation form after each one, with the fifth being observed by a referee mentor who can sign off your 'promotion' or recommend ways to improve your performance.

In short, becoming a qualified rugby referee is nothing onerous; rather, it enhances your enjoyment of this vital part of a coach's skill set by giving you the tools and the confidence required to do the job right; and in doing so, you will help your young players immensely in their development.

8 POSITIONS

Introduction

An adult rugby union team is composed of 15 rugby players and is split into eight forwards (two props, hooker, two locks, two flankers, No. 8) and seven backs (scrum half, fly half, inside centre, outside centre, two wingers and one fullback). In age grade rugby, the situation is different. At the youngest age groups, playing tag rugby, there are quite simply no positions. All players take an equal share in the basic tasks of the game – running (evasion and pursuit), handling, scoring and defending.

From Under 9s upwards, different elements to the game require some different roles to be carried out; but while these roles relate only to certain specific actions in the game, there are still no actual positions for the players to occupy. As still more elements come in, the requirement for specialist roles (props in a scrum, for example) arises, but here a good coach will ensure that all players take a turn at playing these roles. It's only when players get to 15-a-side rugby at Under 13s that the full organisation of a team into forwards and backs finally takes place.

Forwards and backs have very distinct roles on the rugby pitch and, as a result, players will have different physical strengths and weaknesses. Forwards are generally stronger and have a more physical role on the pitch. Backs are known for their running skills, including speed and acceleration, and kicking.

In professional rugby, the line between the physical distinction of forwards and backs is more blurred due to the all-around requirement for strength and speed in the modern game, but in amateur rugby there is more of a clear distinction between these two groups.

Below is a short description of each of the different positions.

FORWARDS
1 Loose-head prop
2 Hooker
3 Tight-head prop
4 Lock
5 Lock
6 Blind-side flanker
7 Open-side flanker
8 No. 8

BACKS
9 Scrum half
10 Fly half
11 Wing
12 Inside centre
13 Outside centre
14 Wing
15 Full back

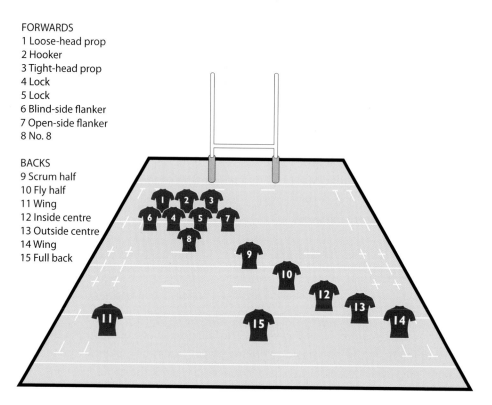

Backs

SCRUM HALF (9)

The scrum half acts as the link between the forwards and the backs. In adult rugby, the scrum half passes the ball out of the scrum to the fly half. A scrum half needs to be quick and have the best pass on the pitch. A scrum half must also have a good vision of the game and be able to control the game. Physically, the scrum half tends to be one of the smallest players on the pitch.

FLY HALF (10)

The fly half acts as the first receiver in the backline. The fly half must be able to pass short and long distances, kick under pressure and have a good vision of the game. The fly half decides what moves the backline will carry on but also involves the forwards into the line, so he must be able to organise the backline and the forwards. A good fly half can win or lose matches.

CENTRES (12, 13)

The inside and outside centres stand between the fly half and the wing in the backline. The inside centre is usually one of the biggest players in the backline and is used as a strong powerful runner to run 'crash balls' straight into the opposition. The outside centre is usually one of the fastest players on the pitch, with a good ability to expose gaps in the opposition's defence. Both centres must be good tacklers and have the ability to work well together with the fly half and wingers to execute moves.

WINGERS/WINGS (11, 14)

The wingers play on the outside of the backline and are usually the fastest players on the pitch (along with the fullback). Their key role is to finish the tries in attack and also stop any breakthrough tries on the fringes. Wingers need to be good under the high ball and work well with the fullback. Wingers can vary in size and can be small and nippy or big and powerful (e.g. Jonah Lomu at 6ft 5in).

FULLBACK (15)

The fullback lines up behind the backline and acts as a sweeper in defence. The fullback must be comfortable under the high ball and have a good strong kick. The fullback must also be able to back himself and launch an attack in isolation from his own try line. Fullbacks must be able to boss the backline as they have the best view of the rugby pitch from behind and work well with the wingers.

Forwards

PROPS (1, 3)

The loose-head and tight-head props work together to form the front row, which refers to their position in the first line of the scrum. Props are usually some of the strongest players on the team as they are responsible for making the big hits, scrumming down, lifting in line-outs and defending the ruck and maul area.

HOOKER (2)

The hooker is positioned between the two props in the scrum. The hooker is key to the set-pieces such as throwing the ball in line-outs and hooking the ball in scrums. The hooker is usually a shorter and smaller player, which makes him easier to support in the scrum; however, he is usually one of the quickest forwards players and has good strength and mobility.

LOCKS (4, 5)

The two locks form the second row, which refers to their position in the second line of the scrum. The locks are usually the tallest players on the pitch and are lifted in the line-outs. They are the powerhouse of the scrum and must have excellent scrummaging technique.

FLANKERS (6, 7)

The open-side and blind-side flankers are positioned on the outside of the scrum and are known for their ferocious tackles off the scrum and mid-match. Flankers are usually some of the fastest and most mobile forwards, known for their strength, fitness and physicality.

NO. 8 (8)

The No. 8 is the last player in the back of the scrum and is charged with controlling the ball in the scrum. The No. 8 is usually one of the most powerful runners with the ball, which he is able to use when picking the ball up from the back of the scrum and running with it. The No. 8 must also have excellent position awareness for scoring tries from the base of the scrum and must be a good tackler.

There are other variations of rugby, including rugby league, rugby sevens and touch rugby, which are not covered in this book in detail. However, the position descriptions are similar across all different forms of rugby. For example, props tend to be strong players on the pitch that are more involved in the contact area of the game, whereas wings are the faster players on the pitch.

In England, rugby league tends to be played in the North of England and rugby union is played in the South. Rugby league is more popular in Australia and New Zealand.

9

BASIC SKILLS

Decision-making

Rugby may look like a sport that is all physicality and brute strength. Power and contact skills, together with evasion, are often the elements that coaches and commentators mention the most. The occasional show of individual skill and flair will be the thing that gets the coverage; but at the heart of every great game and performance is a massive amount of another skill that is critical for the game. That skill is decision-making – the thought processes of a player or group of players that enable them to do the right thing at the right time in the right part of the pitch and at the right time in the game.

A decision to kick for the corner over taking an easy 3-point penalty might be the sort of thing that someone who watches a game of rugby could identify as one such example, but every tackle, ruck, maul, scrum or line-out is littered with decisions.

Does a player step out of a defensive line to make a tackle? Do the players to either side know what to do if that happens? How many players do you commit to a breakdown? Where is the space we discussed in earlier chapters and what's the best way to attack it?

All of these decisions will be made on a rugby pitch. Sometimes the players think about them but often the decisions will be made 'automatically'.

Roughly speaking, this is the pathway from not knowing what to do in a situation (and doing the wrong thing) to the other end of the equation where you instinctively do the right thing without really thinking about it – you just know that that is what needs to be done.

Decision-making like that doesn't just happen – even for the very best players in the world. It is a long process of putting the hours in, doing the practice, making the mistakes and learning from them.

In order to learn from mistakes, you have to make them – and this is where an unstructured playing approach to training really does make a difference. Players should be able to experiment, try stuff out, learn from the good, discard those things that don't work and hone the skills and the decision-making around it.

Evasion

Rugby can be seen as an evasion sport. Evasion is best explained as the ability to move into space using speed and agility. Often described as 'balanced' running, the skills involve changing direction and pace while maintaining balance.

The side step, or the ability to wrong-foot a defender and make them stop or incorrectly guess where you as a runner are going, is part of this skill set.

Young players will benefit from linking the game of rugby to the games they play in the school yard. Tag, It and Stuck in the Mud are all training grounds for this skill.

This will be discussed in greater depth in Chapter 10 (Attack).

Passing

SHORT PASSES

Short passes are one of the most devastating passes in the game, often referred to as an offload. These are covered in more detail in Chapter 10, but we will look at the actual skill in this chapter.

In order to deliver a short pass, a player needs good ball control. This is a pass often just placed in the air in front of a support runner without the need for any power to be put into the pass.

The pass is made predominantly with the fingertips or, at most, with a wrist motion. It is often called a 'pop pass' because the ball pops into the air.

Passing the ball to players in space

Sequence of short passes

Demonstration of passing technique

LONG PASSES

Long passes are more of an active skill as these involve more physical skill. Obviously, the pass needs to go backwards but cover a good distance. These passes can be spun so the ball torpedoes through the air to a wider receiver, or in a similar way to a pop pass but with more power. The ball is often easier to catch in this manner.

Both passes can be worked on in the following exercise:

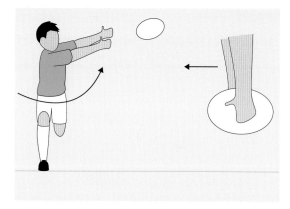

Body position for passing the ball off the ground

DRILLS

Drills are small exercises in spaces set out by coaches, which look to focus on a particular skill. The RFU's view of drills is that it is better to allow players to play the game and the coaches to observe and question, analyse and, if necessary, correct activity. However, drills still have their place and setting up a 'technical area' beside a game is often a great way to focus a few players on a specific skill while the game progresses.

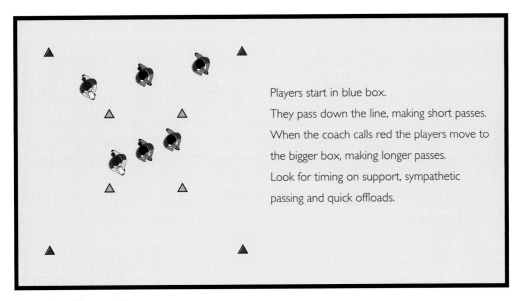

Players start in blue box.

They pass down the line, making short passes.

When the coach calls red the players move to the bigger box, making longer passes.

Look for timing on support, sympathetic passing and quick offloads.

Blue and red boxes drill

Set up a small area beside a pitch and take the opportunity to pull a few players out of the game to focus on set skills. This, coupled with a planned coaching session, allows for focus on individual players together with team skills.

Passing game to practise and reinforce skills

Catching

Hands up in front to give a target for the ball being passed

CATCHING PASSES

Often viewed as a simple skill, catching is the fundamental task in rugby. If a player doesn't catch a pass, he gives the ball away. The catcher or receiver can make the task easier for himself and for the player making the pass by following a few simple steps.

Firstly, the catcher should have his hands up and pushed out towards the ball carrier (communication is helpful, too). This action turns the catcher's chest slightly towards the ball carrier, which in turns helps to straighten his running line and stop him drifting away from the pass.

This means that with hands up, fingers spread, thumbs touching, slightly turned towards the direction of the pass and making eye contact with the ball carrier, the catcher stands the very best chance of catching the pass.

CATCHING KICKS

As the game progresses through the age groups, kicking comes into play and is explained in more detail below. However, as kicking happens, so does the opportunity to catch a kick. Currently, this is an area in the professional game that is under review as collisions in the air are a matter of concern in relation to the safety of players. However, let's look at the skill of catching the ball.

Body position for catching the ball in the air. Turn toward the tryline with knees and elbows up and commit to the catch

- Firstly, the catcher needs to attack the ball in the air by jumping towards it, keeping his eyes on the ball and turning slightly so that if he drops the ball it goes back towards his line and doesn't result in a knock-on.

- The catcher's hands need to be extended and raised, both to grasp the ball cleanly and to allow him to pull it towards him as he catches it.

- As he jumps, it is useful to raise a knee and an elbow. This will result in a strong body position in the air and also as he lands.

- If the catcher is playing in an age group where he can call a mark if he makes a clean catch in the 22, he should ensure he is aware of where he is as he lands and call loudly to request this from the referee.

- If the catcher is looking to counter-attack from the catch, he must ensure he completes the catch first of all.

You can practise this skill with your team's kickers as they practise their kicking. You can progress this practice by adding kick chasers, who will put the catcher under pressure.

Kicking

Kicking is normally allowed from the Under 11s age group onwards in most countries. Games at this stage are restarted (or started) with a drop kick. With the exception of a fly hack (kicking the ball on the ground in open play), the full range of kicks (drop, grubber, place and from hand) is allowed. The fly hack is allowed from the Under 13s age group onwards.

A team that has no kickers not only misses out on the opportunity to gain valuable points, but is at a disadvantage throughout the whole of a match. Most teams have players who can kick the ball but every team has one or two players who are more consistent kickers.

One of the things that make a good kicker is the ability to kick accurately under tremendous pressure. The RFU has published a useful document entitled Maintaining Kicking Effectiveness Under Intense Practice Conditions, which discusses how to increase a player's kicking effectiveness under pressure (http://www.rossrugby.co.za/uploads/skills/maintainingkickingeffectivnessunderpressure.pdf).

If a team has a reliable kicker, they do not have to rely on scrums and can have the kicker put a kick in the corner to put the opposing team under real pressure; or they can have the kicker convert a penalty and put more points on the board, thereby rewarding the rest of the team who have worked hard to force the error from the opposing team in the first place.

Fly hacking the ball on the ground

Drop kick technique

Every rugby player, whether forward or back, can benefit from having a good kicking ability – kicking skills are not reserved for the fly half and fullback only. The better a team can kick and the more players they have with this ability, the more effective they can be in gaining a tactical advantage over their opponents.

There are different kinds of kicks – some gain a team points, some an advantage in terms of yardage.

KICK-OFF

For a kick-off, the main rule is that the ball must go forward at least 10 metres. The kicker has three options when kicking:

- Long kick to try to put the opposing team under pressure;
- Short kick to try to get a teammate to take the ball and possession; or
- Kick to the opposing team's 22, which puts pressure on the opposing player to try to kick the ball away.

Please see below for more information about drop kicking.

PENALTY KICKING

Penalties will happen in every game of rugby and if a team has a kicker who converts the majority of these, it takes the pressure off the rest of the team to score tries because it is possible for a team to win a game through penalties only.

Penalty kicks are generally awarded for offside and foul play.

GOAL KICKING

Like penalties, conversions are a very important aspect of the rugby game and a good goal kicker can make a big difference in a match. Place kicking is one of the hardest skills to perfect, but with constant practice and dedication it can turn into a player's most valuable skill.

A consistent goal kicker is able to contribute to points, demotivate the opposition, make the opposition more careful at the ruck (giving the other team the advantage) and energise his team when rewarding the team's efforts with points.

DROP KICKING

The drop kick is the only way you can score points in a match without the opposition making any mistakes. The drop kick is used for restarts and for drop goals.

Drop goals are always seen as a dramatic end to a match, and in most cases they are. A converted or missed drop goal impacts heavily on the match. Drop kicks can be crucial, especially in professional rugby, as evidenced by Ronan O'Gara's drop kick to give Ireland the win in the Grand Slam and the Triple Crown in 2009.

Drop goals can also be converted if a team feels that they may not get a try and have no chance of moving nearer to the try line.

POSSESSION KICKING

This is the trickiest type of kicking because if a kicker gets it wrong he can give away not only possession but also the advantage the rest of the team has worked so hard to gain.

Possession kicking includes kicking the ball forward to put the opposition under pressure and hoping they drop the ball near their try line; or kicking to a teammate, which results in the opposing team not being able to tackle the teammate before the try.

If the ball goes behind the line used to mark what would be the 22-metre line on a full pitch and is kicked out on the full from there, the line-out is taken from where the ball was kicked. But if the kick bounces into touch, the line-out is taken from where the ball went into touch. As the Under 11s and Under 12s normally play on half of a full-sized pitch, this line is usually marked at around 10–15 metres from the try line.

Scoring a try

A try is scored when a player touches the ball down inside the opposition's in-goal area between the try line and dead ball line. This will result in the scoring team gaining 5 points, and if the conversion is successful then the team will gain an additional 2 points, bringing the total to 7.

When approaching the line, it is important for players to maintain their concentration so as not to lose control of the ball. Players should aim to score tries as near to the posts as possible because the closer the try is made to the posts, the easier the conversion is for the kicker, which can result in the team gaining extra points. This is especially important if the teams are well matched or if your team is having difficulty putting points on the board because of a strong defence. In such a case, kicking could be the key to winning the match and the team with the most conversions and penalty kicks will have a better chance of winning the game.

Of course, if a team has a very good and accurate kicker and the players and coach have confidence in his ability, then scoring a try in the corner is no problem.

Grounding the ball to score a try

DIVING

Sometimes a player needs to dive over the line with the ball if he is on the verge of being tackled and the dive will ensure that he crosses the line and gets the try. However, the dive has also been used by some players as a way to show off to the crowds.

If the ball is touched down correctly then there is technically no problem with diving, but if a player tries to show off and drops the ball then not only can it look rather stupid but it can also cost the team the win. Sometimes this is referred to as 'showboating'.

As you can see in the diagram, it is better to dive downwards rather than upwards. This is because when a player dives downwards he has more control of the ball and therefore less chance of dropping it.

Correct diving technique

Also, when he dives upwards he is in a position where he has less control over his body, so when he hits the floor he has less chance of putting the required pressure on the ball to the ground for the try to be awarded.

There are many examples of videos online showing players being over-confident, needlessly diving and dropping the ball in the process. This is embarrassing and had the players safely placed the ball down rather than dive, they would have scored the try.

However, sometimes diving is required in order to avoid being stopped by the opposition. Great footwork and the ability to dive will serve any winger or fullback very well.

10 ATTACK

There are two very distinct aspects of the game in its most basic form – 'Attack' and 'Defence'. We will look at Defence in greater detail in the following chapter, but broken down into the simplest of explanations, attack is what players do as a team when they have the ball and defence is what they do as a team when they do not.

Rugby as an evasion sport

The first thing most parents think of when considering rugby is that it is a physical contact sport. This is often the first concern for allowing their offspring to be involved in the game. The perception is that the game, even at Under 7s and Under 8s, is the same game as they see on the TV involving the international teams. However, while there are elements of contact in the game, in reality it is an evasion sport. At the outset of the game in the Under 7s and Under 8s age groups, the tag game encourages evasion, replicating the games children play in the playground at school.

Taking a very simple view of the game, when a team kicks off and a player catches the ball, his team moves the ball down the pitch, using passing skills, support running, evasion and speed, to score a try. What happens next is that the opposition kicks off again and the process is repeated. So in very basic terms a player never wants to go into contact if he can help it.

ATTACKING SPACE

So he attacks space. A phrase often used in rugby – but what does it mean? Well, space is where defenders aren't. This can be because they are out of place, either by mistake or because as a team you have created a situation that has put them out of place.

This can be done by players running at angles to interest defenders or commit them to making a decision to attempt to tackle that player, as they expect them to get the ball. If all the attacking players run straight, it is easy for a defending team to match them and ensure that there are no gaps. However, if a support runner heads towards the player carrying the ball, the defender marking them might step in. If the defender doesn't, it is an easy run for the ball carrier through that space. Alternatively, if the defender does, a pass out wider will see the ball carrier in front of the gap left by the defender stepping in.

Gaps can be very small – for example, the space right beside the tackle. This space is the most precious on the pitch – no massive passes, no fantastic handling skills, just a pop pass a few centimetres away from the defender, something that relies on the timing of the support runners.

Drill 1 – hands grid

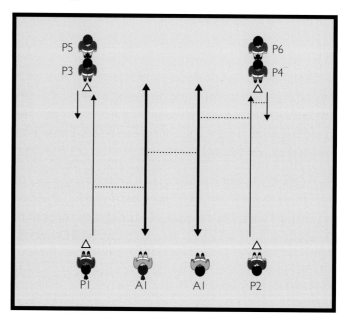

PLAYERS/EQUIPMENT

- 8 + players
- 1 ball
- 4 markers

DESCRIPTION

- P1 starts with the ball, runs forward and passes to A1, who passes to A2.
- P2 receives the ball and passes to P4 running in the opposite direction.
- A1 and A2 must touch the ground between the cones, turn around and receive the next pass.
- A1 and A2 are under constant pressure to catch and pass, turn and get back into a position to receive the next pass.

COACHING POINTS

Pass ball out in front of the player.

- Player receiving pass should have hands up ready and facing passer.
- No spiral passes are allowed.
- Verbal communication is important.
- Stay running straight, particularly A1 and A2 as they tire.
- Keep the work rate high.

VARIATIONS/PROGRESSIONS

- Change direction of the grid to ensure players are passing from both sides.
- Increase or decrease the size of the work area (grid).
- Increase the number of players and balls involved.
- Increase speed – set targets for number of passes in a designated time period.

Drill 2 – 2 v 1 grid

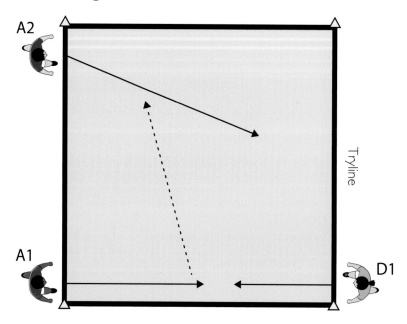

PLAYERS/EQUIPMENT

- 6+ players
- 1 ball
- 4 markers

DESCRIPTION

- In a 5m x 5m grid, two attackers (A1 & A2) start on the side of the grid, attacking one defender (D1).
- The activity begins with the defender (D1) passing the ball to the attacker (A1) who immediately attacks in the grid with the support player (A2).
- They must score at the end of the grid, past the defender D1, without being touched or making an error.
- Once the try is scored, everyone changes roles and the activity starts again.

COACHING POINTS

- The ball carrier should attempt to run at the face or the side away from the support player in an attempt to make him commit to the ball carrier.

- The support player should run at 'space' but should be moving forward when receiving the pass.
- If the defender commits to tag the ball carrier, then the ball carrier should pass.
- The ball carrier can go himself if the defender does not commit.

VARIATIONS/PROGRESSIONS

- Increase to 3 v 2 once players are confident with the 2 v 1.

'Space and evasion' is the key skill that coaches most need to instil in their players. As such, it's sensible that this is the first aspect we coach. Evasion is key for tag rugby. When a player gets 'tagged' (a velcro tag is removed from his belt) he has to pass, and after a set number of tags the ball is turned over. Speed, agility, running lines and all of those technical phrases just mean players can see space and attack it. Add this to the first aspects of handling skills, ball in two hands, passing and catching, and you have the foundation of rugby. A fast-paced game with lots of tries scored and a massive amount of involvement from the small-sided games.

- -

Drill 3 – pass, get back, pass

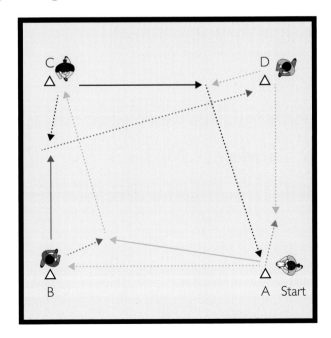

PLAYERS/EQUIPMENT

- 5 + players
- 2 balls
- 4 markers

DESCRIPTION

- A starts with the ball and passes to B who immediately passes ball back to A who is running towards B. A then cuts the corner of the grid and passes the ball to C.
- B then runs to C and receives a pass back from C and then passes to D.
- C runs to D etc.

COACHING POINTS

- Players should have hands up (fingers spread) ready for the ball.
- Communication – call for pass.
- Soft hands and correct passing style (i.e. pop pass or lateral pass).
- Pass ball across the body and point fingers to target after passing.

VARIATIONS/PROGRESSIONS

- Change direction of the grid to ensure players are passing from both sides.
- Increase/decrease the size of work area (grid).
- Increase the number of players and balls involved.
- Increase speed – set targets.

Drill 4 – catch and pass 2 v 1 + 1

PLAYERS/EQUIPMENT

- 4 + players
- 1 ball
- 4 markers

DESCRIPTION

- A1 and A2 aim to beat D1 and D2.

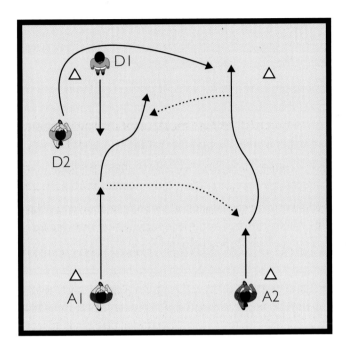

- Activity starts when D1 passes the ball to A1, who advances into the grid with the aim of beating D2, who is now a defender.
- A1 runs forward and commits D1, then passes to A2.
- D2 must run around the cone and attempt to stop A2 and A1.
- A2 then makes an inside pass to A1 if required.

COACHING POINTS

- Foot speed off the line to take the space.
- Attackers to commit defenders by attacking shoulders and providing space for the support players.
- Catch and passing skills under game-related pressure.
- Vision and decision-making under pressure.

VARIATIONS/PROGRESSIONS

- Increase the size of the grid.
- Limit the style of pass allowed (e.g. no spiral passes).

COACHING THE TACKLE

Mini rugby covers the age groups from Under 9s to Under 12s. These age groups see the gradual introduction of the other skills needed for the game.

Tackling, rucks, mauls, scrums and line-outs are introduced in stages, with the tackle being the first step. The stages at which the various skills are introduced are subject to changes from the governing bodies, so it is best to check the actual steps at the time of reading this; but one of the key points to remember is what the point of the Under 7s and Under 8s age groups is.

One of the biggest frustrations we have as coaches is seeing all of the hard work and effort of the Under 7s and Under 8s age groups completely ignored for the first four weeks of the new season as coaches who are new to the game or to coaching encourage players to 'smash' tackle shields. All the running into space and evasion skills are forgotten as coaches and players focus on contact and contact alone.

Why? Well, the RFU regulations have now compressed the training of this element of the game into a period of four weeks to safely teach young players how to safely carry out the core skills of tackling, rucking and mauling. The new regulations and the last few versions of the New Rules of Play (the rules for the Under 7s to Under 12s age groups) expressly forbid the coaching of tackling to this age group until the start of September of their Under 9s season.

Players are often walked through a tackle from a stationary position on their knees to a situation where the attacker is running towards them. This is the area where we believe things start to go wrong. By teaching players to tackle 'passive' attackers, coaches programme those attackers to run straight into the defenders. The same programming happens as soon as a tackle shield is brought into play.

The players with the tackle shield (who should be representing attacking players) either stand still or move up in a straight line. Tacklers need to move and players who are attackers need to see and attack space!

However, as parents, coaches and observers of this transition over a good number of seasons, our opinion remains that the vast majority of these players look forward to the contact aspect of the game and see it as the start of playing 'real' rugby. Well, real rugby isn't just tackling, nor is it just running into space. The joy of the game is that it is a mixture of the two. There is a skill in communicating this to young players and to new coaches who were formerly front row forwards and think that a good contact session is what the players need.

The coaching, therefore, also needs to be a mixture of the two elements: evasion and contact. Players who are behaving as attackers for an exercise need to look for and attack space, while defenders must not assume that attackers will run in a way that will almost assist in making the tackle.

Drill 5 – one out

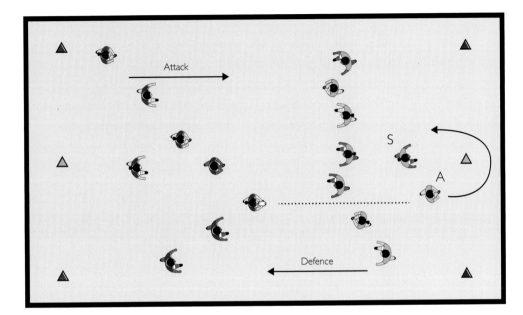

PLAYERS/EQUIPMENT
- 6 + players
- 1 ball
- 6 markers

DESCRIPTION
- The size of the field is changeable to accommodate the number of players.
- If teams are uneven, the coach may elect to run a defensive sweeper (marked S on diagram) to create even numbers in the attack v defence.
- Defenders effect a tackle with a two-handed tag. Once the tag has been made, the defender (A) must turn and run around the marker before re-joining the defensive line.
- When tagged, the ball carrier touches the ground with the ball and passes to continue the game.
- A turnover occurs when the attacking team knocks on and there is no advantage to the opposition.
- A defender running around the back marker cannot take part in play until they have turned the marker.

COACHING POINTS

- Communication – with the defender effecting the tag having to run around the back marker, the defensive team will have one less player, thus creating extra numbers for the attack. The defensive team must communicate and understand a general defensive pattern/structure to combat this mismatch in numbers effectively.

- See space – the attacking team will need to understand and implement key factors of using the ball to capitalise most effectively on the mismatch. Key factors are alignment, angle, speed, support and penetration. Depth of quick realignment is critical.

- Patience – the nature of the game does not mean that the attack must attempt to score off every phase. Control, patience and positive attacking attitudes are required.

VARIATIONS/PROGRESSIONS

- The game can work and training objectives can be met using as few as three players on each team.

- Alternative techniques for ball presentation by the ball carrier, once tagged, can be used before the game continues e.g. turn and pop, go to ground and place, go to ground and roll back.

- Coach may dictate a number of players to be involved in the breakdown situation and count down ball delivery.

- Various degrees of contact could be incorporated once techniques have been coached and effectively demonstrated by the players, e.g. one on one tackles, breakdown situation at the tag (a support player and second defender may challenge for possession).

- -

Drill 6 – breakout

PLAYERS/EQUIPMENT

- 10 + players
- 2 balls
- 14 markers

DESCRIPTION

- Attackers (A1–A4) attempt to score a try over the outside boundary line of the grid set out by the markers. The attackers may attack any side of the grid.

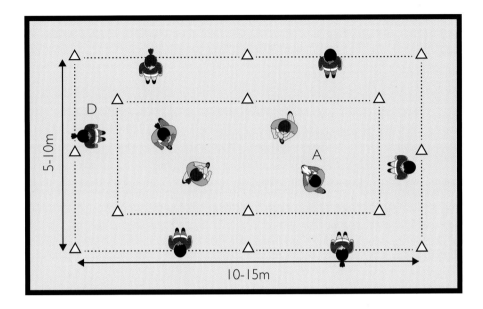

- Defenders (D1–D6) must remain within the boarded area.
- Defenders perform two-handed tags to stop attacker.
- Attacking players are to move the ball around in the aim to create/find a gap between the defenders to score a try.
- A point is scored when an attacker scores a try without being tagged.
- The coach may put a time limit on how long the attackers have to score as many points as possible.

OBJECTIVES/ COACHING POINTS

- Develop communication in defence.
- Promote skills of committing a defender to create space.
- Develop quick and effective decision-making skills in attack.
- Ensure area is large enough for number of players.
- Stress importance of vision to avoid collisions.
- Communication in attack and defence very important.
- How is space/gaps created? Angle and speed of run and pass important.

VARIATIONS/PROGRESSIONS

- With greater team numbers, add an extra defender to each end (the grid then becomes a square approximately 10–15m) and add extra attackers.
- Begin with one ball, then progress to two.
- Introduce contact with the aim of involving skills of switch, screen pass, circle ball to support player. If attacker is stopped and does not get away a pass immediately, then the attackers must attack a different side of the grid.
- Increase the number of defenders.
- Decrease size of grid to increase pressure.

- -

Drill 7 – zone ball

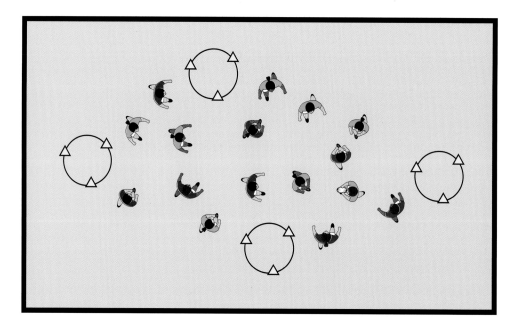

PLAYERS/EQUIPMENT

- 10 + players
- 1 ball
- 12 markers

DESCRIPTION

- Two teams play in the area displayed in the diagram.
- One team begins with the ball and attempts to score points by having one team member catch the ball in one of the goal zones outlined by the markers.
- The attacking team (A1–A8) cannot run with the ball and each player has 5 seconds to pass the ball to a teammate once in possession.
- Attacking players cannot stand in the goal zones, but must enter the zone just before receiving the pass to score a point. Once a point is scored, the same team continues with the ball and must attack another zone.
- The defending team (D1–D7) pressures the opposition and must keep an arm's distance from the ball carrier.
- A turnover occurs when the ball is dropped or a pass goes to ground.

COACHING POINTS

- Attacking players must utilise space and/or create space to play the game effectively.
- Attacking players work to commit defenders using speed and angle of run to create space for a supporting teammate.
- Communication is critical to the effectiveness of both attack and defence.
- The techniques involved in the progressions of the game need to be recognised and practised before implementation.
- The challenge game can be used as a warm-up activity (beginning with the game described above and moving into the progressions once the body is warm and some stretching has been performed) or as a conditioning activity.

VARIATIONS/PROGRESSIONS

- The attacking team can run with the ball. The opposition attempts two-handed tags to halt progress of the attacking team. Once tagged, a turnover occurs.
- Once tagged, the attacking team must take a passive grip on the ball before passing to a teammate to continue play. The attacking team has four tags before a turnover occurs.
- Once tagged, the attacking team must perform a grip and drive on the ball carrier before continuing the play. The attacking team has four tags before a turnover occurs.
- Three passes must occur before a point can be scored in the goal zone.

At this stage the game starts to resemble adult rugby. It becomes 15 a side on a full-sized pitch and at Under 16s level, with the addition of lifting in the line-out, the game is all but the same. The younger age groups play shorter games but here is where the unit skills such as the scrum and line-outs come to the fore. Players start to specialise in positions.

In the mini and midi age groups, players are encouraged to try all of the positions and not end up pigeonholed, as they change shape massively over this period. This is where coaches need the skills from the Scrum Factory course to build an eight-player scrum that works as a unit.

Game-related training

Children learn things better by doing them. One of the best coaches we know says that the less he talks during a session, the better that session is. So set the players an objective, let them play, and then ask them how things went. The results will surprise you. They see the issues most of the time and, if not, a few well-placed questions will encourage them to suggest ideas for improvement.

Drill 8 – straight running

PLAYERS/EQUIPMENT

- 4 + players
- 1 ball
- 5 markers
- 16 agility poles

DESCRIPTION

- A1 sprints through the agility poles/markers (gates) and passes to A2.
- A2 catches the ball before the agility poles, runs through them then passes to A3 after the poles and then A3 passes to A4 in same way.
- After A4 runs through the poles, A4 runs around the first cone and places the ball.
- All the attackers continue to pick up then place the ball until the second cone.
- On the second cone, the attackers realign, calling which gate they have, i.e. 1, 2, 3 or 4.
- Person on gate 1 holds until all are set and then begins again.

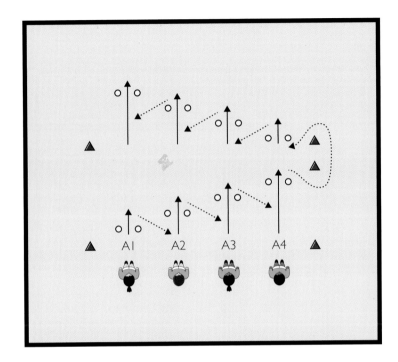

COACHING POINTS

- Treat the poles as gaps in a defensive line. Players must be able to get through these cleanly.
- Hands up, ready for the balls.
- Run straight – the players shouldn't have to change direction to get through the poles.
- Players should aim to build up to sprinting pace while catching and passing.
- If there are too many dropped balls, slow the pace down.
- A1 shouldn't loop around in support until A3 has received the ball, etc.
- Players need to look where they are.

VARIATIONS/PROGRESSIONS

- Vary the distance between the gates (agility poles).
- Change the skill in between the cones, i.e. inside support.
- Have a halfback pass the ball in to A1.
- Replace gates with single poles that act as defenders. Players will need to change their running angle either in or out.

Drill 9 – 3 v 2 – straight running and cutting down the space

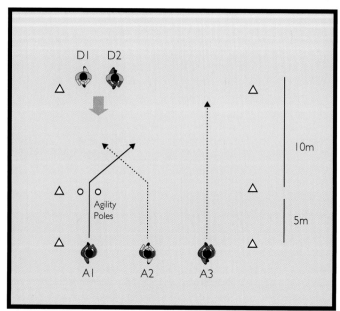

PLAYERS/EQUIPMENT

- 5 + players
- 2 balls
- 6 markers
- 2 agility poles

DESCRIPTION

- A1 accelerates at full pace straight through agility poles. A1 is not allowed to change angle of run until after the agility poles.

- A2 and A3 accelerate at full pace and can't change angle of run until they have passed the middle cones.

- The two defenders (D1 and D2) start on the cone and must communicate to get across to cover A1 and A2.

- D1 and D2 cannot move forward until A1 has reached the agility poles.

- Attackers can run hands or progress to plays familiar to the team.

COACHING POINTS

- A1 should be accelerating through the agility poles.
- D1 and D2 must move forward quickly to cut down the attackers' space.
- Hands should be able to beat the defenders.
- Defenders must stay on the attackers' inside shoulders.
- A1 should aim to commit at least one defender.
- Defenders should aim to force the attackers wide to beat them.
- Two-handed grab to start.
- Activity should be worked on from both sides so the players are working on passing L to R and R to L.
- Attackers should be committing defenders by attacking shoulders.

VARIATIONS/PROGRESSIONS

- Increase or decrease the size of the grid.
- Attackers only allowed to run a set move (i.e. switch) and A1 must hit the open runner.
- Move on to 4 v 3.
- Increase the contact, i.e. tackle.

Drill 10 – grid target passing

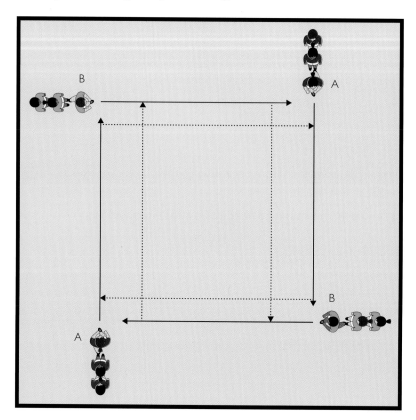

PLAYERS/EQUIPMENT

- 8 + players
- 2 balls
- 12 markers

DESCRIPTION

- Set up a grid 5m x 5m and line up players as indicated in the diagram above.

- While working in one grid, players are split into two even groups who work together, i.e. As with As and Bs with Bs.

- A1 and B1 start activity by running forward with a ball. When they get to a marker, they must pass the ball across the grid to their partner, i.e. A1 passes to B2 and B1 passes to A2.

- The grid continues with A2 then running forward and passing across the grid to B3, and B2 doing the same but passing to A3.
- Continue.

COACHING POINTS

- All lateral passes need to be put into space for the support player to run on to (attack) the ball.
- Players should have hands up ready for the ball and should begin with outside foot forward to initiate straight running.
- Players work to have all lateral passes consistent while attacking with speed and running straight. Passing speed needs to be maintained.
- Players need to communicate by calling for the ball when they are in a position to receive it.
- Groups need to work hard to realign, ready for the next run through.
- The grid can be used as a warm-up activity, gradually increasing the intensity as the body warms up.
- Quality of pass (speed and direction).

VARIATIONS/PROGRESSIONS

- Organisation of grid can be modified to suit player numbers.
- Grid size can be altered (larger or smaller).
- Change ball (football, tennis ball, etc.).

As coaches, we prefer to use games to practise skills, rather than drills. One of the best games for handling space identification is called 'Parramatta touch'. Three teams works well, two of five and one of six. The team of six are the attackers and the two teams of five are defenders. Have a pitch set up where the attackers start in the middle and the two defending teams defend either end of the pitch. The attackers have an extra player, a readily created overlap. They attack one end at a time. If the ball is dropped, knocked on or a player is tackled, then they turn and attack the other end.

Drill 11 – Parramatta touch

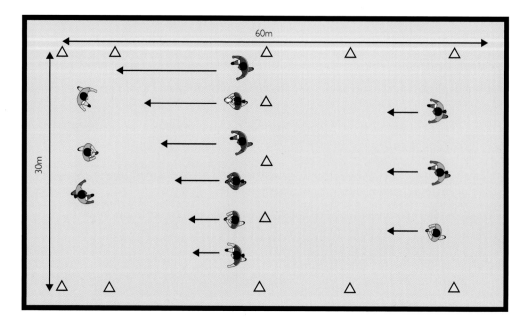

PLAYERS/EQUIPMENT

- 8 + players
- 1 ball
- 13 markers

DESCRIPTION

- Attack starts from the centre cones, and attacks one defensive zone. Attack only gets one chance to score.
- If this occurs, or a touch is made, dropped ball, forward pass etc., the attack turns around and immediately attacks the far zone. This continues for a set time dictated by the coaches.
- If the attack scores, the defence must run around the centre cones and get back to their defensive zone before the attack starts attacking them again. If defence make a touch, they get a rest.
- The defenders cannot defend outside of their zones.
- Each team gets 10 attacks – add the scores.

COACHING POINTS

- Lines of running must be effective in order to score.
- Attacking a drift and blitz defence.
- Realignment is essential in order to be effective continuously.

VARIATIONS/PROGRESSIONS

- Organisation of grid can be modified to suit player numbers.
- Grid size can be altered (larger or smaller).
- Set target for tries scored.
- Vary numbers of attacker/defenders.

The Parramatta touch is a fast-paced drill, looking at running lines and support play for the attacking team. Communication is key, as is running from depth and identifying and exploiting space.

This can be expanded to focus on defensive skills such as running drift defence plans and further expanded to introduce tackles and quick rucks.

Supporting runners

Support runners are players who as yet have not got the ball but might be passed to as play progresses. At times, these are the players who create the spaces, even without the ball. If you watch the most successful teams play, you will see that the ball carrier often has two or three runners close to hand who can be passed to.

Think back to tag rugby and the idea of not coming into contact with the ball.

The support runners are the ones who offer the offload (short pass) options or are there to secure the ball in a ruck or a maul if a tackle is made.

In order to fully utilise support runners, it works best if the ball carrier has options to either side. This allows the ball carrier to pass either way if tackled but also acts as an immediate group of players to work to recycle the ball should a tackle be completed.

OFFLOADS

Offloads or short passes are the most destructive of all passes.

Offloads are small passes to support runners. These are made in the course of the tackle by the defender, which takes that player out of the game. Often passes over just a few centimetres, these get the attackers beyond the defensive line.

A series of these passes can be very effective, creating chaos within the opposition's line and opening opportunities to score. As these passes do not create a breakdown, they force the defending team to continue to retreat to stay onside.

The offload requires commitment from the ball carrier together with carefully timed involvement from the support runners.

Basic drills

The basic moves (aimed at mini rugby players) range from switch, miss and loop to create overlaps to more complex moves with two- or three-phase plays.

Often in mini rugby, players will pass down the line from one player to the next, with little variety. This makes it easy to defend, as the opposition can work out where the next pass is going and also number up against the attackers.

SWITCH

A move such as a switch is effective because it confuses the defending team. The ball carrier runs towards a defender and a support runner across the ball carrier's path at 45 degrees (imagine a pair of scissors). The ball carrier then turns away from the support runner and passes the ball back to him. This, in effect, is done out of sight of the defenders as the ball is shielded behind the ball carrier. The advantage of this is that if there is a possibility of this 'move' being made, the defender may step early to the player whom they perceive will have the ball, thereby leaving a space.

- -

Drill 12 – simple switch

PLAYERS/EQUIPMENT
- 6 + players
- 1 ball
- 4 markers

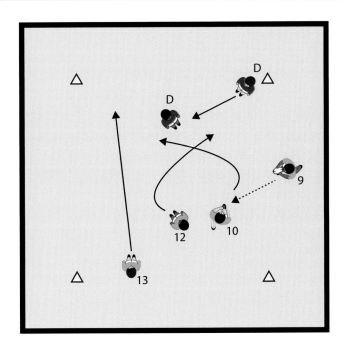

DESCRIPTION

- Set up a grid 20m x 20m.
- Designate four attack players and two defence players.
- One attacker (9) starts with the ball at the edge of the grid, ready to feed to teammates.
- The other attackers line up ready to play 3 v 2 against the two defenders.
- The aim is for the attack to switch the direction of play to wrong-foot the defence.
- Defenders can tag/touch or tackle as desired.

COACHING POINTS

- 10 runs initially at the inside shoulder of the defender opposite to attract his attention, then cuts across towards the next defender out, drawing the first defender with him.
- 12 runs initially at the outside shoulder of his man, before swerving sharply, crossing behind 10 to attack the space created inside the first defender.
- 13 runs hard at the space outside the second defender, calling loudly for the ball to create uncertainty in the defence.
- Switch pass from 10 to 12 happens behind 10's body, shielding the ball from the defenders' view.

VARIATIONS/PROGRESSIONS

- For beginners, run the move unopposed at a slower pace.

- Increase to 4 v 3, giving each attacker a defender to mark them.

- Try the move at walking pace, asking the attackers to observe and comment on how the defenders react – what options can they suggest?

- Increase attackers to 5 using a wider grid and allow them to experiment with options – switch between 12 and 13, switch and inside pass to 9, dummy switch and give to 13 etc.

- Ensure players rotate between attack and defence and try out each role in the attacking team. This is an opportunity for the ball carrier to 'dummy' the pass – that is, not pass to the support runner and go through the gap himself.

Drill 13 – simple dummy pass

PLAYERS/EQUIPMENT

- 5 + players

- 1 ball

- 4 markers

DESCRIPTION

- Set up a grid 20m x 20m.

- Designate three attack players and two defence players.

- Coach (C) starts with the ball at the edge of the grid, ready to feed to players.

- The other attackers line up ready to play 3 v 2 against the two defenders.

- The aim is for the attacker 12 to deceive his opposite defender by faking a pass to 13, creating a gap for 12 to go through.

COACHING POINTS

- 10 runs at the inside shoulder of the defender opposite to 'fix' him and feeds the ball to 12.

- 12 runs initially at his man's inside shoulder, then changes his line to the outside shoulder, drawing the defender with him.

- 13 runs in support calling loudly for the ball, taking a line just outside the defender to attract his attention.

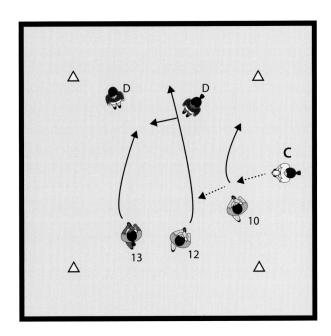

- 12 fakes a pass to 13, causing the defender to move across to cover 13 and leaving a gap for 12 to exploit.

- 12 must carry the ball in two hands to suggest he will pass, and look at 13 as he dummies the pass ('lie with your eyes').

VARIATIONS/PROGRESSIONS

- For beginners, run the drill 3 v 1 at a slower pace

- Allow attackers to choose where to throw the dummy (e.g. at 10, 12 or 13). Which option do they take and why?

- Ask the attackers to perform it at walking pace and get them to observe and comment on how the defenders react

- Increase defenders to equal the attackers (e.g. 3 v 3) or overload the defence (3 v 4) to challenge the attack further

- Experiment with dummy switches and combination moves

- Ensure players rotate between attack and defence and try out each role in the attacking team.

MISS-PASSES

Miss-passes are a simple way to move the ball wider and faster. The ball carrier misses the support runner immediately beside him and passes instead to the next support runner. Normally a method to stretch the defence, this needs a good pass over a longer distance. In order to practise this, the distance on a pass needs to be considered together with the timing of the support runners.

Drill 14 – simple miss-pass

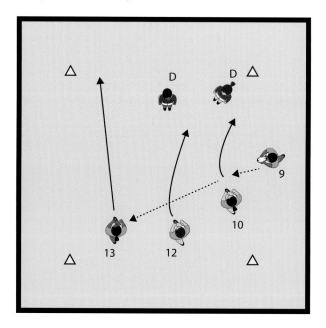

PLAYERS/EQUIPMENT

- 6 + players
- 1 ball
- 4 markers

DESCRIPTION

- Set up a grid 20m x 20m.
- Designate 4 attack players and 2 defence players.

- One attacker (9) starts with the ball at the edge of the grid, ready to feed to teammates.
- The other attackers line up ready to play 3 v 2 against the two defenders.
- The aim is for the attack to get the ball wide to the 'wing' so he can exploit the overlap out wide and score.

COACHING POINTS

- 10 and 12 run at the inside shoulders of the defenders opposite to 'fix' them.
- 9 feeds the ball to 10 who passes beyond 12 to 13, who has come up quickly, while…
- 12 runs hard at his man, keeping eye contact and calling loudly for the ball to create a diversion.
- Once ball gets to wing in space, allow players to play on and respond to what they see.
- Attackers should ensure they line up with depth to reduce risk of long pass being intercepted.

VARIATIONS/PROGRESSIONS

- For beginners, run the drill unopposed and at a slower pace.
- Increase to 5 v 3, allowing attackers to choose where to throw miss-pass (i.e. from 10–13 or 12–11). Which works best?
- As 11 attacks space outside, last defender will race across to try to stop him; this creates space inside, so how will attack exploit this?
- Increase attackers to 6 using a wider grid and ask for 2 miss-passes to get the ball wide. What do they notice about how the defence reacts?
- Ensure players rotate between attack and defence and try out each role in the attacking team.

LOOP

Loop passes provide an opportunity to outnumber the defenders. The action is best described as a 'wrap around'. The ball carrier passes to the immediate support runner and loops behind them and into the attacking line outside the new ball carrier (or into a wider position). This creates an overload in attacking players.

- -

Drill 15 – simple loop pass

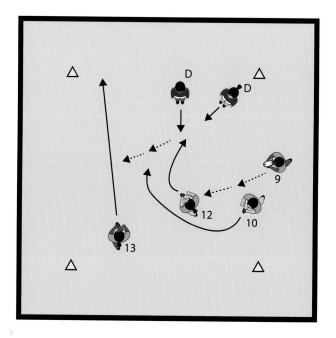

PLAYERS/EQUIPMENT

- 6 + players
- 1 ball
- 4 markers

DESCRIPTION

- Set up a grid 20m x 20m.
- Designate 4 attack players and 2 defence players.

- One attacker (9) starts with the ball at the edge of the grid ready to feed to teammates.
- The other attackers line up ready to play 3 v 2 against the two defenders.
- The aim is to create an extra man in the line by one player looping round his teammate to take a return pass.
- Defenders can tag/touch or tackle as desired.

COACHING POINTS
- 9 feeds 10 who immediately feeds 12 outside him.
- 12 runs initially at his man; on receipt of the ball he moves back inside to attack the gap between his defender and the one inside.
- After passing to 12, 10 runs round behind and up alongside him to take a return pass, now attacking the space outside the second defender.
- 12 now feeds 13, who attacks the space at speed with 10 in support.
- Timing is crucial; 10 must not make his looping run until after he has given the ball to 12.

VARIATIONS/PROGRESSIONS
- For beginners, run the move unopposed at a slower pace.
- Increase to 4 v 3, giving each attacker a defender to mark them.
- Try the move at walking pace, asking the attackers to observe and comment on how the defenders react – what options can they suggest?
- Increase attackers to 5 using a wider grid and allow them to experiment with options – loop between 12 and 13, 12 misses 10 and passes straight to 13, etc.
- Ensure players rotate between attack and defence and try out each role in the attacking team.

11

DEFENCE

Defence can be broken down into: (1) what an individual player does in defence and (2) what units (or groups) of players do in defence.

Tackling

One of the core skills of defence is the tackle and teaching this safely is paramount. With the New Rules of Play, which are described in detail in Chapter 7 (Rules), the tackle is introduced in mini rugby at the Under 9s age group.

This is often coached from a static kneeling position, one on one, with a static ball carrier to help a player to understand the basic mechanics of this skill.

Below is a simple tackle progression checklist for the side-on tackle:

1 Ball carrier kneels – tackler kneels (only for side-on tackle to demonstrate head position)
2 Ball carrier stands – tackler kneels (encourage leg drive)
3 Ball carrier walks – tackler on one knee
4 Ball carrier stands – tackler squats
5 Ball carrier walks – tackler squats
6 Ball carrier walks – tackler walks
7 Ball carrier runs – tackler runs

With the youngest age groups, it helps to embed the correct tackling technique by teaching and continually reinforcing the following sequence:

- 'Eyes to thighs' – helps the tackler to focus on the target area.

- 'Cheek to cheek' – the tackler needs to put his face alongside the runner's backside to get his head in the right position.

- 'Shoulder in' – the shoulder should make contact first instead of the hands.

- 'Ring of steel' – players should be taught to keep their arms spread until they hit the runner, then wrap them round tightly to stick to the runner and bring him down.

Body positions in the tackle

The idea is to ensure the correct placement of the tackling player's head so as to avoid raised knees etc, and to ensure the tackling player puts a strong 'circle' of arms around the ball carrier and takes him to ground in a safe manner. As a contact sport, this element of the game is very carefully managed. The initial tackle training is normally focused on a side-on tackle but in a game there are two other tackles that occur regularly – (1) the head-on tackle and (2) the tackle when chasing a player.

Head-on tackles at pace demand bravery and commitment and are excellent examples of where a transfer of skills from other sports can pay off. These tackles are often not a demonstration of strength but more of the techniques seen in martial arts such as judo, where you use the opponent's own speed and strength against him to bring him down.

Here is an example of good tackling technique:

- Foot speed off the line – Defenders should be coached to move off the line quickly, in order to cut down the time and space available to the ball carrier. This will increase pressure on the ball carrier. A split stance (one foot forward and the other back) in defence should be implemented to encourage defenders to move off the line quickly.

- Approaching from a shoulder – This allows the defender to take the space on one side of the ball carrier, allowing him to attack in one direction only. It is commonly coached to push up on the inside shoulder to allow the defender to drift once the ball has been passed. The momentum of the defender would be going in the same direction as the ball for a lateral pass.

● Foot placement into contact – It is extremely important to coach your players to get a foot into the 'hula hoop' (an imaginary hoop around the feet of the attacker) just prior to contact. One school of thought suggests that the lead foot should be the opposite foot to the tackle shoulder. This enables the tackler to have his centre of gravity closer to the target, and thus exert more power. However, more important is that the lead foot must be 'to or through' the target. This means placing the lead foot as close as possible or past the feet of the ball carrier. This enables the tackler to remain balanced in contact as well as provide a strong leg drive.

Tackle training session

Judo training to help with contact skills

- Head up and eyes open – The tackler must keep his head up and eyes open so that on the point of contact, or just prior, he can react to any change that the ball carrier implements, e.g. step, pass, etc.

- Square hips – The tackler should have his hips and shoulders facing forward to keep the ball carrier in his 'strong tackle zone'.

- Angle of tackle – This aspect of the tackle is aided by the approach. The emphasis on creating an angle to the ball carrier depends largely on the distance between tackler and ball carrier. On an extended distance, the tackler should avoid a direct front-on tackle, but instead make contact at about 45 degrees to exploit the weak spot of the ball carrier and knock him off his running line, while still going forward.

When implementing the tackle, it is important to take the following coaching points into consideration:

- Head placement – Eyes open, chin up and head to the side of the ball carrier. It is important to keep the head in line with the spine and have the head as close to the target as possible. This will allow the shoulders a good contact with the ball carrier.

- Contact point on ball carrier – The tackler should target the thighs or shorts of the ball carrier and implement the squeeze to the thighs to prevent continued forward movement.

- Strong arm, wrap and squeeze – Initial contact will be made with one shoulder, arm and chest (broad contact area) and therefore it is important that the contact is dynamic and strong. This can be achieved by using a flexed arm from wrist to shoulder. Arms should finish as close as possible to linking to each other. The squeeze component allows the tackler to stick to the ball carrier, effectively executing the tackle.

- Foot speed in contact – After the lead foot is 'to or through' the ball carrier and contact is made, the tackler should use small dynamic steps to aid in chasing the initial contact (hit). This will provide leg drive in contact. While the ball carrier is going backwards, he is not in a position to provide a clean ball presentation.

- Contesting the ball at the tackle contest – The tackler should aim to regain his feet after taking the ball carrier to ground (important to position himself on top) and dominate the space above the ball and over the tackled player to contest possession.

Chasing a player and making a tackle is another skill again. This can be in the form of a tap tackle, where the tackler in effect 'taps' the foot of the running ball carrier into his leg, causing him to trip over his own feet. This is often a last-chance attempt to stop the ball carrier.

A tap tackle technique is very different from a side-on tackle or front-on tackle. The checklist is below:

- The tackler is within arm's reach of the ball carrier.
- The tackler aims to 'tap' one of the ball carrier's feet, usually by diving.
- The tackler hits with an open palm and knocks one foot into the other, causing the ball carrier to stumble.
- The tackler should ensure his head is not close to the feet of the ball carrier as he makes the tap.

Tap tackle

The tackler has a responsibility to put the tackled player on to the ground under control. If the ball carrier's hips are taken higher than their shoulders, the tackler runs the risk of being sent off. Once the tackler has put the ball carrier on the ground, he must release the ball carrier and roll away. The tackler has to make a 'clear release' – let go of the ball carrier, get to his feet and only then can he contest for the ball.

The following are two drills that can be used to teach young players tackling skills:

Drill 16 – tackle square

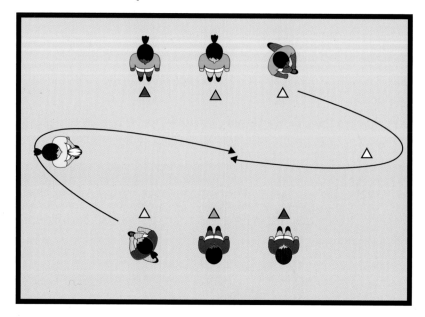

PLAYERS/EQUIPMENT

- 6 + players
- 1 ball
- 6 markers

DESCRIPTION

- Basic tackle practice 1 v 1.
- Players on a coloured cone, tacklers on one side and ball carriers on the other.
- Coach calls a colour and players on that cone on each side react. Ball carrier runs to one end and takes the ball from the coach, runs down the middle of the channel and the tackler meets them and makes the tackle.

COACHING POINTS

- Look for body position in contact.
- Arms locked around ball carrier and head position.
- Look at speed into contact, controlled and reacting to ball carrier.
- Look at matching players for size, pace and strength initially.

VARIATIONS/PROGRESSIONS

- This can be started at walking pace with the ball carrier taking only a direct route from coach to far cone.
- Progress to allow ball carrier to use evasion skills so tackler has to react and realign.
- Add second defender (delayed run) to contest the ball once the tackle is completed.

Drill 17 – 3-point tackle drill

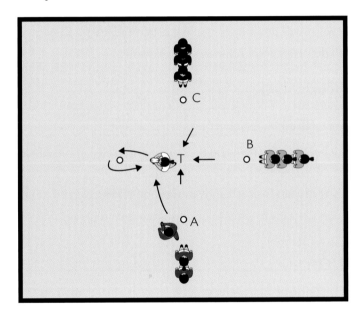

PLAYERS/EQUIPMENT

- 5–15 players
- 1 ball
- 3 markers

DESCRIPTION

- A single attacker starts at (T), runs around the pole and heads back to (T).
- A defender from marker (A) makes a side-on tackle on the attacker at (T).
- The defender completes the tackle by getting to his feet, dominating the space over the ball.

- The defender picks up the ball and becomes the attacker. He runs around the pole, runs back towards (T) and is tackled by a defender from marker (B), in a front-on tackle.
- The defender from (B) completes the tackle by getting to his feet, dominating the space over the ball. He then picks up the ball and becomes the attacker, running around the pole and being tackled in a side-on tackle by a defender from marker (C).
- Continue until all players have had a turn in all positions.

COACHING POINTS

- Players to remain safe by adopting safe head position and appropriate body position.
- Leading foot as close to the attacker as possible (inside a hula-hoop around the player).
- Contact made with chest and shoulder moving forward into contact.
- Use leg drive to propel attacker sideways or backwards.

VARIATIONS/PROGRESSIONS

- The coach calls defenders forward from any of the three markers (A, B, C) rather than following the circular anticlockwise pattern.
- Open the space between the pole and the markers to make it more difficult for the defender to get close to the attacker and to improve the defender's tracking skills.
- Attackers working in pairs to practise cleanout of defender or rip.
- Defenders working in pairs to practise buddy tackle (two-man tackle).

Organisation

Those are the individual aspects of defence for players. However, rugby is a team game and defence is a unit/team skill. This is seen in two ways. One is that defence is defensive – nothing more than a period of play where the team without the ball looks to stop the team with the ball from scoring. The other is that it is the quickest way to retrieve the ball. This depends on the mindset of a coach. However, within those two approaches the basic unit skills have much in common.

Defence as a team depends on organisation, support, and one of the core values mentioned elsewhere in the book – TEAMWORK.

Coaching defensive organisation – and indeed a player understanding it at the very outset of his rugby journey – can be difficult; however, at its heart it can be broken down into the sorts of games children play in the park or the school playground, without the input of coaches.

Think of the variety of games where one team attempts to run from one side of the area to another. If the 'defending' team works as individuals and all pick out different runners, the structure of their defence doesn't work. If they stay as a line, 'connected' to the nearest two of their teammates, they make the 'attacking' runners' jobs very difficult.

So in the organisation of a defence, if the players can work as a line almost connected by an invisible piece of rope, you have the first, most basic structure needed for defence.

- -

Drill 18 – controlling the line

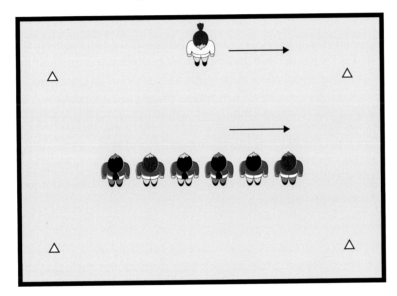

PLAYERS/EQUIPMENT
- 6 + players
- 4 markers

DESCRIPTION
- Basic line organisation drill.
- 6 players form a line, looking at the coach.
- Coach indicates using signals, left/right/advance/retreat.
- Players work together to maintain the line and gaps and communicate with each other.

COACHING POINTS

- Look for players to maintain the distance between themselves.
- Look to see that the line is maintained so no gaps appear.
- Encourage lots of communication in the line, both between individual players and across the whole team.

VARIATIONS/PROGRESSIONS

- Instead of a coach indicating, add two players and one ball and the line reacts to when the ball is picked up and passed.
- For further progression, identify which defender is engaging the ball carrier and complete tackle.

Communication is one of the biggest elements in defence and if, as a team, the players talk during this period of the game, it will provide massive benefits. But communication needs to be worthwhile. Players shouting random words such as 'tackle' isn't much use. Someone calling the line forward is a good idea. So the player nearest to the tackle area could take that role, calling the team to go forward as the attacking side moves the ball from the tackle area.

Players in the line need to talk to the players to their left and right – almost as if working with a group of three, but if all players work with the person to their left and right then the line is connected. Talk between these players can be seen as 'little talk', communication to organise small units within the line.

The 'big talk' commands the line speed, the pace at which the defensive line moves forward. It also includes the communication about where the ball might be. If the player in front of you has the ball, communicating that loudly to your team informs them that you have the ball carrier and have become the tackler in that moment and also lets the ball carrier know you have him. It might put doubt in his mind.

So working together in a line at a pace that works for all and communicating with each other is critical.

In order to practise this, there are some simple drills to ensure that connection and line speed are aligned with some communication. As a young team, that real win comes in defence if players hold the structure of the line and don't all gravitate to the ball, leaving space elsewhere on the pitch. Remember, space is the area any attacking team wants to find, so gifting this is the thing the defending team needs to avoid.

Drill 19 – defence line activity

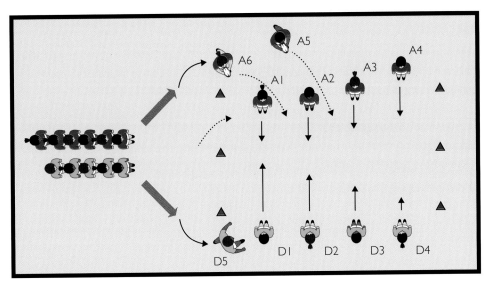

PLAYERS/EQUIPMENT

- 11 + players
- 1 ball
- 6 markers

DESCRIPTION

- Set up a grid 30m x 10m.
- 6 attackers (A) vs 5 defenders (D)
- On the coach's call, the attackers and defenders run around opposite cones and begin attacking and defending.
- Attackers and defenders must align on the run.
- The ball is passed in from the middle cone to A1.
- After one phase, the drill starts again from the other side of the grid.

COACHING POINTS

- Attackers and defenders must communicate to realign.
- Defender needs to align off the markers with shape (half a step behind the closest inside defender) and line up on the inside shoulder of their opponent.

- Line speed to ensure pressure is applied to the attacking team (limited time and space).
- Hustle line for all inside defenders, push hard and cover inside channel of the current ball carrier.
- Jam line on outside of ball carrier, defenders will need to remain as square as possible. This will allow the outside defenders to provide assistance in the tackle or to cover the outside channel to the current ball carrier.

VARIATIONS/PROGRESSIONS

- Increase the number of attackers/defenders and include the tackle contest (breakdown) defensive structures.
- Continue activity for a designated time.

We will look at a few progressions of the defensive line now. This is often where terms come into the game and you might have heard about 'drift defence' or 'blitz defence'. These defensive structures can be a bit advanced for young players just coming into the game, but we will have a quick look at the very basic elements.

DRIFT DEFENCE

A drift defence uses communication and the touchlines as the core of its structure. The defender in front of the ball carrier is the person in charge of the line and calls the commands for this style of defence. They instruct the line to 'drift' – all move across – to either left or right as the ball carrier makes the pass. This approach pushes the attacking team wider but ensures that, as a defensive line, you maintain the ratio of defenders to the number of attackers.

As a defender pushes the attacker wide, the touchline comes into play. From a defending point of view, defenders can use both touchlines – after all, if the ball carrier crosses it, the defending team gets the ball back.

BLITZ DEFENCE

The 'blitz' defence relies on speed and puts the attacking team under pressure as their time to think and space to do anything faster is reduced. The idea is to push front as a defensive line very quickly and close the space between the defence (at the onside line/in line with the tackle) and the ball carrier.

If we now break down defence to children who have started playing rugby and so play tag rugby, it is very much like the games we mentioned earlier in this chapter. The playground

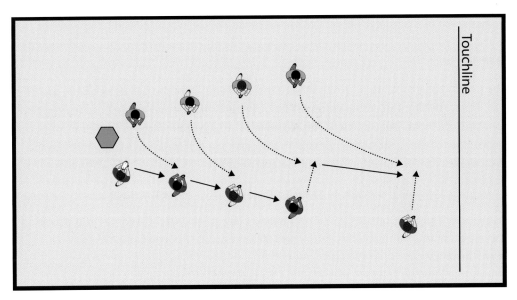

Touchline

Drift defence

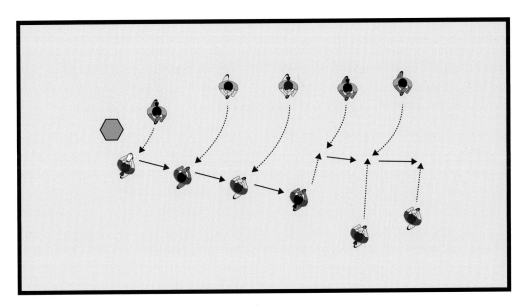

Blitz defence

games come to the fore. A 'tackle' is made as the defending player pulls the tag from the belt of the ball carrier. This also creates the imaginary line on the pitch at which the defending team line up.

The tackling player has to return the tag to the ball carrier and the ball carrier must pass the ball. This is the simplest of 'breakdowns'/tackle areas. In this game, the defence team's role is to restrict the possible gaps for the attacking team, to make the tag and force the attacking team either to use up all of their passes (in the early age groups) or to make a mistake and drop the ball, which turns it over to the defending team.

So the structure and the ability to make a tag is key at this very early stage.

As the age groups progress, the skill of the tackle (see page 144–145) comes into play. In this aspect of the game, the ball carrier and tackler both have responsibilities. As we have seen, the tackler must put the ball carrier down safely and this element of the game will be closely managed by coaches and referees. The tackler must then release the ball carrier and make an effort to roll away from the tackle area. The ball carrier must release the ball, either passing or placing it. When the tackle is first introduced at the youngest age group, this is the extent of the progression. Another player from the attacking side then moves in to pass the ball away.

As the game progresses, the tackle area becomes a contest for the ball and this also needs to be included in the defensive structure. At Under 10s, the structure is made up of the tackler and the ball carrier plus one more player from each team. If the ball carrier is taken to ground, this becomes a 'ruck'; if the ball carrier stays on his feet, it is called a 'maul'.

The following drills can be used for practice and progression in defensive training sessions. All of these drills are suitable for all levels from minis upwards, although the approach to explaining them will need to be adjusted depending on the age group. In addition, with the Under 7s and Under 8s, the 'tackle' would be a tag rather than a full tackle.

Drill 20 – continuous tracking/defence drill

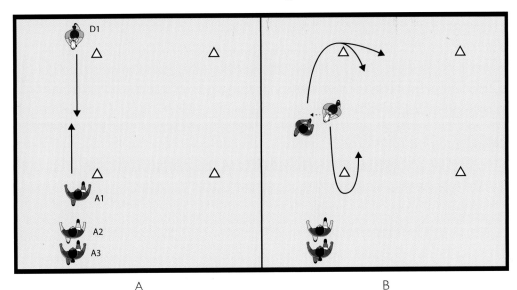

A   B

PLAYERS/EQUIPMENT

- 2 – 10 players
- 1 ball
- 4 markers

DESCRIPTION

- Defender D1 starts with the ball. On the coach's cue A1 and D1 run towards each other, D1 pops the ball to A1 on the way past.
- Both players round the opposite markers. A1 then attempts to score at the original starting end. At the same time D1 attempts to move up and put a two handed tag on A1.
- A1 passes the ball to A2 and then becomes a defender.
- D1 lines up with the attackers.
- Once players have had a turn at defending or attacking they continually rotate.

COACHING POINTS

- Players should perform attack and defence roles at pace.
- Attackers initial movement should be forward to commit defenders (three quick steps).

- Defenders should be encouraged to move up quickly to deny time and space to the attacker. The defender should also defend on the inside shoulder of the attacker, pushing them out.

- In 1 v 1 situation, attackers should attempt to beat the defender with running angles and footwork. While in the 2 v 1, attackers should also attempt to commit (move) the defenders, creating space for support.

- Defenders should never be beaten on the inside.

VARIATIONS/PROGRESSIONS

- Build up the attacking players so it becomes a 2 v 1 situation (as seen in diagram B).

- Build on the number of defenders as well as attackers so there is a 3 v 2 situation. The size of the grid may need to be altered.

- Introduce the tackle in place of the two-hand grab.

- Encourage players to attack inside as well as outside defenders, using angles such as switches.

- For the activity to be more attack orientated use three attackers against one defender. The defender starts with the ball and on the run past the attackers they choose to pass to any of the attackers who then turn and attack.

- -

Drill 21 – defence – numbering up

PLAYERS/EQUIPMENT

- 14 + players

- 6 markers

- 1 shield

- 6 tackle bags

DESCRIPTION

- 7 defenders (D), 6 tackle bags (O) and 1 attacker (A)

- A moves forward and joins the line of tackle bags wherever he wants and continues moving forward.

- As A moves forward, D moves forward and tackles the tackle bags and A.

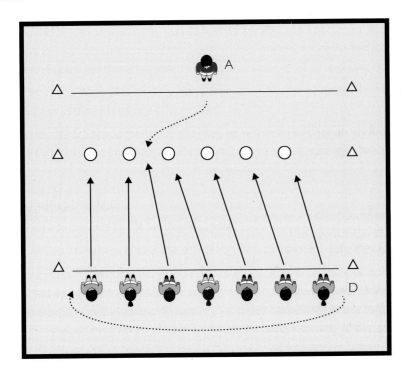

- D must communicate and adjust to where A is coming into the line.
- Every tackle bag and the attacker should be covered.
- After each tackle, the last defender runs to the other end and all the defenders shuffle along one.

COACHING POINTS

- Keep hips square while moving up.
- Communicate which bag you have before moving forward and as A is entering the line.
- Emphasis is on communication and technique.
- As the players become competent, shorten the rest period.
- Players must work to get off the line quickly, balance then accelerate into contact.

VARIATIONS/PROGRESSIONS

- Add more attackers.
- Change the tackle bags for attackers and make them jog in with the other attackers, sprinting into the line from depth.

Drill 22 – 1-on-1 defence drill

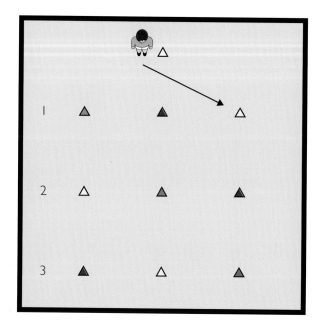

PLAYERS/EQUIPMENT

- 2 + players
- 1 ball
- 10 markers

DESCRIPTION

- A player may act as the tacklee.
- Defender (D) starts on the yellow marker. The coach will nominate a marker to move to in line 1 by calling that colour.
- The coach will then call 'slide', nominating the marker to slide to by calling the colour. E.g., 'Slide green.'
- As the player is sliding, the tacklee should simultaneously be moving towards the defender on an angle either side.
- The sequence is repeated on line 2 and again for line 3.
- The player will complete three hits per sequence.

COACHING POINTS

- As the tacklee is advancing forward, the defender should be encouraged to move off the line.
- The defender should take the space with head up and hands up.
- While taking the space, the defender should remain upright with a last second dip before contact.
- The defender should lead into contact by stepping through, or 'getting a foot up'.

VARIATIONS/PROGRESSIONS

- This drill can be passive, using a shield; or progressive, using a tackle suit.
- Drill can be progressed from initiating a tackle to completing an offensive tackle and contesting the ball.
- Tacklee may use evasion in an attempt to avoid contact.

Drill 23 – 1-on-1 defence – reaction and contact

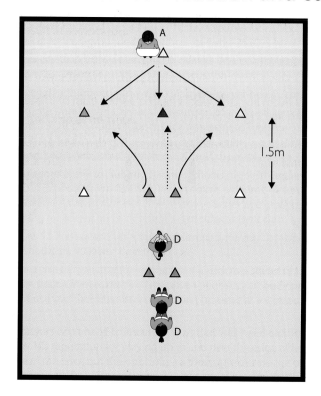

PLAYERS/EQUIPMENT

- 1 + players
- 6 markers
- 1 shield

DESCRIPTION

- One-on-one tackle, where the defender (D) runs quickly to the green markers.
- On reaching the green markers, the shield holder nominates a coloured marker.
- Both attacker and defender meet at the nominated marker, where the defender makes a tackle on the shield with the appropriate shoulder.
- The shield holder is required to attack a shoulder of the defender.
- Once the hit has been made, the defender jogs back around, ready to start again. Each defender makes up to three tackles before rotating.

COACHING POINTS

- Defenders should move at speed through the green markers.
- On approach to the tackle, the defender should shorten stride length but maintain forward movement and quick leg speed.
- When entering contact, the defender should place a foot towards the attacker and concentrate on the position of their head.
- The defender's spine should stay in line with the head to the side to ensure one line of force to effect the tackle.

VARIATIONS/PROGRESSIONS

- Use a contact suit instead of a shield.
- Progress from making the hit to completing the tackle, and putting the man on the ground.
- Vary the type of tackle by having the attacker run at shoulder or running at a wider space.
- Defender gets to feet and secures the ball after the tackle.

Drill 24 – 3-on-3 defensive pattern

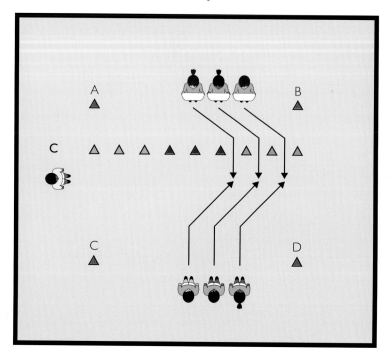

PLAYERS/EQUIPMENT

- 6 + players
- 13 markers
- 3 pads
- 1 contact suit

DESCRIPTION

- Three attackers holding pads line up on the between A&B, three defenders line up between C & D.
- On the coach's (C) call, both defenders and attackers move forward. The coach will then call a colour, either blue, red or green.
- Defenders must react to the coach's call of a colour, at the same time staying in line with the other defenders.
- When setting up the grid, pad holders should have less distance to run than defenders.
- The defenders need to push forward and react by making the tackle.

COACHING POINTS

● On the call 'Go', the defenders should move forward at pace.

● When the colour is called, the defenders should head towards that colour, shortening steps and adjusting for the hit.

● At the same time, the pad holders should move towards the colour called and attempt to square up as they head through the marker.

● Defenders should take a last-second step forward, driving past the contact point.

VARIATIONS/PROGRESSIONS

● The activity may be increased to 4 v 4 or 5 v 5.

● The pad holders may change angle and position.

● Pads may be replaced with suits or attackers may progress to using a ball.

Drill 25 – tackling 1 v 1 with 51% gain

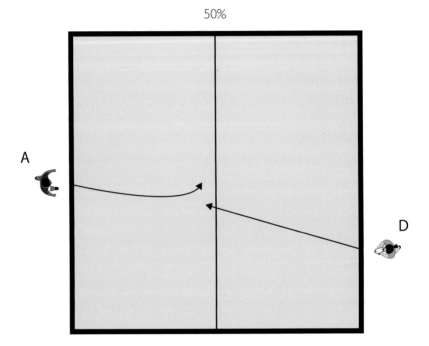

PLAYERS/EQUIPMENT

- 2 + players
- 1 ball
- 4 markers

DESCRIPTION

- In a 5m x 5m grid, an attacker (A) begins at one end and a defender (D) begins opposite at the other end with a ball.
- (D) begins the activity by passing the ball to (A), who is attempting to score a try at the end of the grid past (D).
- (D) must get a two-handed tag on (A) while (A) is trying to gain as much territory as possible (over 50%) and avoid being tagged.
- (D) should position themselves on the inside (one side) of the attacker to dominate and control the attacker's movements.

COACHING POINTS

- The defender should start in a position with one foot forward, ready to run forward to cut down time and space for the attacker.
- The defender will need to accelerate quickly and straight ahead (up one side of the attacker) to gain as much territory as possible.
- Once the defender is approaching the attacker, he will need to change his foot strike pattern to short, dynamic steps to remain balanced and able to change direction quickly if required.

VARIATIONS/PROGRESSIONS

- Increase/decrease the size of the work area (grid).
- Position attackers anywhere across the top of the grid, forcing the defender to react and position himself on one side.
- Have the attackers perform activities (lateral movement, hit the ground, etc.) at the end of the grid, which the defender must copy. The attacker can attack at any stage. The defender will need to react and make a successful tag as far up the grid as possible.

Rucking

Let's look at the ruck first.

Ruck diagram

The idea for the attacking team is clear: move the ball to another player. The defence, however, has a couple of options: slow the attacking team's progress or contest for the ball on the ground. This is where the additional players in the tackle area come into play. If they can move their opposition off the ball by pushing them backwards over the ball from standing over it, they can create a turnover.

Equally, if they make it difficult for the attacking team to make their pass, then the defensive team has time to organise itself: 'little talk' and line speed.

I v I mini-ruck

As the age groups progress, more players are allowed to contest at the ruck and this is where teams have to decide how many players to commit to this contest and when to do so. If a team has a good tackler and a player who is difficult to get out of the tackle area, the attacking team might be forced to commit more of its players to secure the ball and therefore give the defending team an advantage in numbers across the pitch, which in turn creates more pressure for the attacking side. The decision to do this might be a pre-determined play or just the decision of players in defence and communicated to their teammates.

Also, a defending team might decide that the attacking team hasn't secured a ball very well at a ruck. They could communicate this to the players closest to the tackle area and they might all contest the ball, trying to drive the attacking team off it and cause a turnover.

There are numerous elements that can be developed within this part of the game. A coach will talk to players about when to go to ground with the ball, how best to place the ball and give the attacking team the best opportunity to secure and retain possession.

In defence, as the numbers at the tackle area increase, so do the roles and responsibilities. Teams will often put defenders around the tackle area and these are designed both to stop attacks close to that area and to contest the ball or place the first players from the attacking team under pressure.

Presenting the ball

Mauling

If the tackled player stays on his feet, this is seen as a 'maul'. This is not allowed in the tag age groups and a referee will call a tackle and the ball carrier will have to pass the ball. The same is the case in the Under 9s, the first age group where tackling is permitted.

However, from the Under 10s a maul can be formed and this is a very effective attacking platform. The ball carrier stays on his feet and drives forward with the assistance of one of his teammates (in

Maul diagram

I v I mini-maul

the first stages of the game). Once a maul is called, the defending team is not allowed to take the maul to the ground (this is a penalty).

As the age groups progress, more players can join the maul and this becomes a test of both strength and organisation to defend. The attacking team must continue to move forward and a referee will instruct them to use the ball if it stops. If they don't use the ball within 5 seconds after the referee's instruction, the defending team gets the ball in either a scrum or a restart pass.

The final part of defence is turning it into attack. Teams that contest the ball and win it need to know quickly what to do with it and for that you go back to the attack skills covered in Chapter 10. Space is where you want to attack and space is very unlikely to be close to the tackle area in which you have just won the ball.

This is where teams need to align quickly from a flat defensive line into an attacking formation but quick passes away from the tackle area on the turnover is most likely to give the best results.

Set pieces

The 'set piece' in the game covers two main elements, which are covered in more detail below. They are both methods that restart the game following a break in action.

The scrum is used when a ball is knocked forward or passed forward.

The line-out is used if the ball has gone off the pitch 'into touch'.

Scrum

The scrum is where the pack in adult rugby comes together to contest a ball. This is introduced in a staged manner from the Under 9s, where the scrum is not contested.

The scrum is formed in the early stages at three-a-side with the nearest three players to the knock-on. The three players have the roles of two props and a hooker (see Chapter 8 for

Building a scrum

Side view of a scrum

descriptions of the different positions). As the age groups progress, a second row of two locks is added before being joined by a No. 8 and then two flankers.

The eight players are referred to as 'the pack' and they work together to secure the ball which the attacking scrum half puts in the gap between the two front rows (props and hookers).

Line-out

A line-out is used when the ball has gone off the pitch. This is another aspect of the game where the 'pack' is used.

In rugby up to and including Under 15s, lifting is not allowed in the line-out and the two packs form two lines into which the attacking hooker throws the ball from the touchline.

From Under 16s, players can be lifted in the line-out to form one of the most spectacular sights in the game – players held in the air by their teammates, contesting the ball 10 feet (3m) above the ground.

Line-outs are a combination of skill, teamwork and training – and require great trust in fellow players. A line-out is also a great opportunity to challenge the opposition's abilities and to take advantage if it is a weakness in their game.

Lifting in the line-out

Conclusion

Rugby is a wonderful game that can help children and young people learn teamwork and leadership skills, build their confidence, practice discipline and sportsmanship and improve their coordination and fitness. It's also good fun and great way to make friends!

However, in order for children to enjoy playing rugby, coaches, parents, referees and spectators must play their part to create and maintain the right ethos of the game.

Coaches must teach the fundamentals of rugby well whilst keeping players safe and encouraging development. Parents must be aware of their influence and support the coach with the best interest of the player. Referees must control the game at all times to maintain safety for players and make sure that the rules and ethos of the game are being followed.

Finally, spectators must follow the RFU's Code of Rugby and conduct themselves in an appropriate way so that everyone can enjoy the game. All of these roles are vital in order for mini and youth players to succeed at rugby.

We hope this book has given you a good introduction into the game of rugby as a parent or coach. The resources in the following pages will help you with further information on rugby, and please also see our website – www.miniandyouthrugby.com.

See you by the rugby pitch!

RESOURCES

[1] Give It A Try: IRFU Targets Next Generation Of Women's Rugby. http://www.irishrugby.ie/news/32296.php#.VOhhjhy4Ql5

[3] RFU plans to introduce rugby to 100,000 women and girls. http://www.englandrugby.com/news/rfu-introduce-rugby-100-000-women-and-girls/

[4] The International Rugby Board (IRB) changed its name to World Rugby on 19 November 2014 as part of a major rebranding programme.

[5] Rugby's Core Values. http://www.englandrugby.com/about-the-rfu/core-values/

[6] The Code of Rugby. http://www.englandrugby.com/about-the-rfu/core-values/

[7] In the UK, Colts level rugby consists of players under 19 years of age.

[8] School of Hard Knocks on TV. http://www.schoolofhardknocks.org.uk/ontv/

[9] School of Hard Knocks: Pedro's Story. https://www.youtube.com/watch?v=giN_dG77RT8

[10] Limbless Rugby Player Inspires Others. http://fox8.com/2012/06/27/limbless-rugby-player-inspires-others

[11] Moment fed-up spectator trips up flying rugby player in bid to stop junior team conceding another try during 64–5 thrashing. http://www.dailymail.co.uk/news/article-2617018/Moment-fed-spectator-trips-flying-rugby-player-bid-stop-junior-team-conceding-try-64-5-thrashing.html

[12] Bryncoch RFC sign tells parents who take age grade rugby far too seriously: 'It's not the final of the world cup.' http://www.southwales-eveningpost.co.uk/Bryncoch-RFC-sign-tells-parents-kids-rugby-far/story-20846506-detail/story.html

[13] https://www.youtube.com/watch?v=5YUF9LSXAkY

[14] Give It A Try: IRFU Targets Next Generation Of Women's Rugby. http://www.irishrugby.ie/news/32296.php#.VOhhjhy4Ql5

[15] The Disadvantage of Summer Babies. http://freakonomics.com/2011/11/02/the-disadvantages-of-summer-babies/

[16] O'Driscoll has always been grounded, regardless of fame. http://www.irishexaminer.com/sport/rugby/odriscoll-has-always-been-grounded-regardless-of-fame-262093.html

[17] The *Guardian*. 'Concussion: how rugby union's rulers risk the lives of their players' http://www.theguardian.com/sport/2013/dec/14/rugby-union-concussion-medical-experts

[18] Coaches. http://www.englandrugby.com/my-rugby/players/player-health/concussion-headcase/

[19] Following the tragic death from 'second impact' concussion of a schoolboy player in Northern Ireland, the RFU issued a SCAT card (Sport Concussion Assessment Tool) for coaches and First Aid staff to use, to evaluate a player for the effects of concussion and if appropriate, to prevent them from resuming play and being put at further risk.

[20] These age grade regulations apply to club rugby only: schools rugby in England is governed by the England Rugby Football Schools Union (ERFSU), which enjoys a degree of autonomy in regard to making changes to its laws. As at September 2014, many younger age grade players experience one set of rules while playing for school and a different set of rules at their club.

[21] World Rugby Laws: Law 16.2(a) states that 'All players forming, joining or taking part in a ruck must have their head and shoulders no lower than their hips.'

[22] A group of our coaches was demonstrating formation of a ruck to a squad of Under 10s and one placed his hand on the floor. When asked for their observations about body positions, the first thing one of the players noticed was that 'Stan isn't supporting his weight'. A great spot from our future elite ref!

[22] Anyone who thinks players don't need to know the laws that well need only look at All Blacks' captain Richie McCaw. His reputation for playing up to and over the edge of legality doesn't come from ignorance of the laws, but the opposite – a thorough knowledge of the laws and their enforcers, so he knows exactly how far he can push it and get away with it. His achievements as player and captain speak for themselves.

[24] The author is a qualified RFU referee and coach with 10 years' experience refereeing age grade and adult rugby

INDEX